MATH PHONICS™
FRACTIONS
&
DECIMALS

BONUS BOOK–ALL NEW IDEAS

Quick Tips and Alternative Techniques for Math Mastery

BY MARILYN B. HEIN
ILLUSTRATED BY RON WHEELER

Teaching & Learning Company
1204 Buchanan St., P.O. Box 10
Carthage, IL 62321-0010

THIS BOOK BELONGS TO

_____

ACKNOWLEDGEMENTS

Sincere thanks to Adam Hein, Regina Cortner, Joe Gallagher and Jed and Todd Shepherd. Also to Julie Meyer for moving to Alaska and Carol Meyer for visiting her.

DEDICATION

I would like to dedicate this book to my husband, Joe; our children, Gretchen, Troy, Adam, Sarah, Robert, Nick and Jenny; and my parents, Vincent and Cleora Vestring; also to God who gives us all knowledge and every freedom!

Cover art by Ron Wheeler

Copyright © 2002, Teaching & Learning Company

ISBN No. 1-57310-347-0

Printing No. 987654321

Teaching & Learning Company
1204 Buchanan St., P.O. Box 10
Carthage, IL 62321-0010

Math Phonics™ is a registered trademark to Marilyn B. Hein.

TABLE OF CONTENTS

Dear Teacher or Parent,

Welcome to the *Math Phonics™–Fractions & Decimals Bonus Book*! As with the other two bonus books in this series, this book focuses on the more difficult decimal and fraction processes and has all new ideas for classroom demonstrations, new worksheets, activity sheets, wall charts and games. If you have not looked at the other two bonus books, please do so. This book will refer to materials in those books—and also the original six *Math Phonics™* books. All nine books work together to give the math student a comprehensive foundation in the basic math facts and processes.

Take a look at pages 7-16—Place Value Wall Charts and related materials. Also I think you'll really find the Fraction Wall Charts on pages 31-36 useful—they cover basic fraction concepts in new ways. If you like giving a fun page once in a while, look at pages 42, 55 and 61. This book also contains two original games—Cinco on pages 29-30 and Decimal Dice on page 65. With 38 pages of practice work, this book will help your students master fractions and decimals.

I knew one problem with writing this book would be thinking up word problems that would be interesting and have variety. I decided the word problems in the book should center on a trip to a specific location. About that time, I ran into four families that were vacationing in Alaska. I couldn't imagine why anyone would want to go to Alaska—I thought of it as nothing but snow and 24-hour nights during the winter. But it has so much more. A little research convinced me that word problems would be fun to write and read if Alaska was our destination.

The first bonus book focuses on school situations. The second covers a vacation to some generic spot nearby. This one deals with a trip to Alaska. However, all three contain situations that a student could encounter in real life.

I wish the very best to you and all your students and sincerely hope that this book is just what you need to perk up a few students who really need a boost! I truly had fun thinking up all these ideas—I hope you have fun using them!

Sincerely,

Marilyn

Marilyn B. Hein

WHAT IS MATH PHONICS™?

Math Phonics™ is a specially designed program for teaching fractions and decimals or for remedial work.

WHY IS IT CALLED MATH PHONICS™?

In reading, phonics is used to group similar words, and it teaches the students simple rules for pronouncing each word.

In *Math Phonics™*, math concepts are learned by means of simple patterns, rules and wall charts with games for practice.

In reading, phonics develops mastery by repetitive use of words already learned.

Math Phonics™ uses drill and review to reinforce students' understanding. Manipulatives and practice games help reduce the "drill and kill" aspect.

HOW WAS MATH PHONICS™ DEVELOPED?

Why did "Johnny" have so much trouble learning to read during the years that phonics was dropped from the curriculum of many schools in this country? For the most part, he had to simply memorize every single word in order to learn to read, an overwhelming task for a young child. If he had an excellent memory or a knack for noticing patterns in words, he had an easier time of it. If he lacked those skills, learning to read was a nightmare, often ending in failure–failure to learn to read and failure in school.

Phonics seems to help many children learn to read more easily. Why? When a young child learns one phonics rule, that one rule unlocks the pronunciation of dozens or even hundreds of words. It also provides the key to parts of many larger words. The trend in U.S. schools today seems to be to include phonics in the curriculum because of the value of that particular system of learning.

As a substitute teacher, I have noticed that math teachers' manuals sometimes have some valuable phonics-like memory tools for teachers to share with students to help them memorize fraction concepts. However, when I searched for materials which would give students a chance to practice and review these tools, I found nothing like that available. I decided to create my own materials based upon what I had learned during the past 40 years as a student, teacher and parent.

The name *Math Phonics™* occurred to me because the rules, patterns and memory techniques that I have assembled are similar to language arts phonics in several ways. Most of these rules are short and easy to learn. Children are taught to look for patterns and use them as "crutches" for coming up with the answer quickly. Some concepts have similarities so that learning one makes it easier to learn another. Last of all, *Math Phonics™* relies on lots of drill and review, just as language arts phonics does.

Children *must* master basic fraction and decimal concepts and the sooner the better. When I taught seventh and eighth grade math over 20 years ago, I was amazed at the number of students who had not mastered fractions and decimals. At that time, I had no idea how to help them. My college math classes did not give me any preparation for that situation. I had not yet delved into my personal memory bank to try to remember how I had mastered those basics.

When my six children had problems in that area, I was strongly motivated to give some serious thought to the topic. I knew my children had to master the basics, and I needed to come up with additional ways to help them. For kids to progress past the lower grades without a thorough knowledge of those concepts would be like trying to learn to read without knowing the alphabet.

I have always marveled at the large number of people who tell me that they "hated math" when they were kids. I firmly believe that a widespread use of *Math Phonics*™ could be a tremendous help in solving the problem of "math phobia."

WHAT ARE THE PRINCIPLES OF MATH PHONICS™?

There are three underlying principles of *Math Phonics*™.
They are: 1. Understanding
            2. Learning
            3. Mastery
Here is a brief explanation of the meaning of these principles.

1. **UNDERSTANDING:** All true mathematical concepts are abstract which means they can't be touched. They exist in the mind. For most of us, understanding such concepts is much easier if they can be related to something in the real world–something that can be touched.

   Thus, I encourage teachers to let students find answers for themselves using fraction strips and circles, decimal charts and diagrams. I think this helps the students to remember answers once they have discovered them on their own.

2. **LEARNING:** Here is where the rules and patterns mentioned earlier play an important part. A child can be taught a simple rule and on the basis of that, begin to practice with fractions and decimals. But the learning necessary for the basic fraction and decimal concepts must be firmly in place so that the information will be remembered next week, next month and several years from now. That brings us to the next principle.

3. **MASTERY:** We have all had the experience of memorizing some information for a test or quiz tomorrow and then promptly forgetting most of it. This type of memorization will not work for fractions and decimals. In order for children to master them, *Math Phonics*™ provides visual illustrations, wall charts, manipulatives, worksheets and games. Some children may only need one or two of these materials, but there are plenty from which to choose for those who need more.

MATHMATICAL CONCEPTS

HOW TO MAKE PLACE VALUE WALL CHARTS

MATERIALS: 22" x 28" tagboard, four small envelopes—3¾" x 6½", laminating pages, play money—pages 11-16, 24 3" x 5" index cards, black permanent marker, colored dry-erase marker

DIRECTIONS

1. Seal the flaps on the envelopes. Cut them in half so that each half measures 3¾" x 3¼". Use seven of the halves.

2. Choose one of the place value charts—money or decimal fractions.

3. Turn the tagboard with the 28" side along the bottom.

4. Glue or tape the seven half envelopes with their lower edges 11" from the bottom of the tagboard and arranged as pictured on the chart you chose.

5. Letter all the titles and labels above and below the row of envelopes with the permanent marker.

6. For the money chart, copy pages of play money and play coins.

7. For the decimal fractions chart, cut the 24 3" x 5" index cards into thirds. Write 10 on 10 of them, 1 on 10 of them, .1 on 10 of them, .01 on 10, etc.

8. Cut 2" x 2" squares of laminating film. Place one square in the center of each envelope.

ACTIVITIES

1. Teacher or student volunteer writes a number on the board—perhaps $1254.36 if you are using the money chart. Another student must write each digit on the correct envelope with the dry-erase marker and put the correct play money in each envelope.

2. For the decimal fraction chart, teacher or student volunteer writes a number on the board—perhaps 25 and 367 thousandths. Another student must write the correct digit on the correct envelope with the dry-erase marker and put in the correct cards from the decimal cards.

3. Erase the digits with a tissue and repeat.

4. Copy a wall chart for each student or group of students. Give each one a vinyl page protector and dry-erase marker. Read a number; student writes each numeral in the correct box.

5. The large number labels chart (page 10) can be enlarged, laminated and used as a wall chart or copied for each student's math notebook.

BASE 10 SYSTEM
MONEY PLACE VALUE

TEN THOUSANDS	THOUSANDS	HUNDREDS	TENS	ONES	AND	TENTHS	HUNDREDTHS
10,000	1000	100	10	1		$\frac{1}{10}$	$\frac{1}{100}$
10^4	10^3	10^2	10^1	10^0	•	10^{-1}	10^{-2}
$(10 \times 10 \times 10 \times 10)$	$(10 \times 10 \times 10)$	(10×10)	(10)	(1)		DIMES	PENNIES
						$\frac{1}{10^1}$	$\frac{1}{10^2}$

BASE 10 SYSTEM—PLACE VALUE
DECIMAL FRACTIONS

AND

TENS	ONES		TENTHS	HUNDREDTHS	THOUSANDTHS	TEN THOUSANDTHS	HUNDRED THOUSANDTHS
10.0	1.0	.	.1	.01	.001	.0001	.00001

BASE 10 SYSTEM LARGE NUMBERS

In 1987 the estimated population of the world was—
4,975,000,000 people.

The commas separate this number
into groups called "periods" with different labels.

UNITS — NO SPECIAL LABEL	THOUSANDS	MILLIONS	BILLIONS
ONES	ONE THOUSANDS	ONE MILLIONS	ONE BILLIONS
TENS	TEN THOUSANDS	TEN MILLIONS	TEN BILLIONS
HUNDREDS	HUNDRED THOUSANDS	HUNDRED MILLIONS	HUNDRED BILLIONS

Population can be read: 4 billion 975 million people

Penny ¹/₁₀₀ of a dollar $ .01	**Penny** ¹/₁₀₀ of a dollar $ .01	**Penny** ¹/₁₀₀ of a dollar $ .01	**Penny** ¹/₁₀₀ of a dollar $ .01
Penny ¹/₁₀₀ of a dollar $ .01	**Penny** ¹/₁₀₀ of a dollar $ .01	**Penny** ¹/₁₀₀ of a dollar $ .01	**Penny** ¹/₁₀₀ of a dollar $ .01
Penny ¹/₁₀₀ of a dollar $ .01	**Penny** ¹/₁₀₀ of a dollar $ .01	**Dime** ¹⁰/₁₀₀ = ¹/₁₀ of a dollar $ .10	**Dime** ¹⁰/₁₀₀ = ¹/₁₀ of a dollar $ .10
Dime ¹⁰/₁₀₀ = ¹/₁₀ of a dollar $ .10	**Dime** ¹⁰/₁₀₀ = ¹/₁₀ of a dollar $ .10	**Dime** ¹⁰/₁₀₀ = ¹/₁₀ of a dollar $ .10	**Dime** ¹⁰/₁₀₀ = ¹/₁₀ of a dollar $ .10
Dime ¹⁰/₁₀₀ = ¹/₁₀ of a dollar $ .10	**Dime** ¹⁰/₁₀₀ = ¹/₁₀ of a dollar $ .10	**Dime** ¹⁰/₁₀₀ = ¹/₁₀ of a dollar $ .10	**Dime** ¹⁰/₁₀₀ = ¹/₁₀ of a dollar $ .10

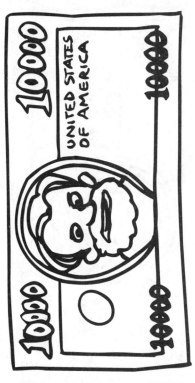

16

SUMMARY OF THE 10 BASIC STEPS

1. Reviewing Basic Computational Skills

This is a pre-assessment step to determine if students have the skills needed to work more difficult fraction and decimal problems.

2. Reviewing Basic Fraction Skills

This step assumes that students have already been introduced to the basic fraction skills. If they have not, use *Math Phonics™—Fractions* to introduce those skills. If so, use these pages to brush up on those skills.

3. Addition & Subtraction of Fractions with Regrouping

Math Phonics™—Fractions barely touched on regrouping. This step explains this in more detail.

4. Multiplication & Division of Fractions with Cancelling & Mixed Numbers

Cancelling will be presented as reducing before multiplication. Students will practice more difficult problems using mixed numbers.

5. Understanding the Base 10 System

Students will learn place value labels and how to read and write numbers which include decimal fractions.

6. Reviewing Basic Decimal Skills

Basic decimal computational skills were presented in *Math Phonics™—Decimals*. Those skills will be reviewed and pre-assessed in this step.

7. Adding & Subtracting Decimal Fractions

Students will work on more difficult addition problems and learn to put in a decimal when a number does not have one.

8. Multiplying & Dividing Decimals

Students will review rules for placement of decimals in multiplication and division problems and practice this skill.

9. Fractions, Decimals, Ratios & Percents

Simple percent ratio problems, sale prices and simple ratio word problems will be taught.

10. Rules, Games & Assessments

There will be a summary page of rules and games followed by assessment pages.

LESSON PLAN 1: REVIEWING BASIC COMPUTATION SKILLS

OBJECTIVE: Review and assess students' basic computational skills which will be needed in order to work fraction and decimal problems.

MATERIALS: math notebook for each student, practice pages from the other eight *Math Phonics*™ books as needed, math troubleshooting page (page 19), basic facts page (page 20), math phonics rules pages (pages 21-25), pre-assessment pages (pages 26-27)

DEMONSTRATION: Here are two possible ways to approach this unit.
1. Give the assessments first and then decide what each student needs to study.
2. Go over the *Math Phonics*™ rules, have students drill each other with flash cards from other Math Phonics books and the math facts page (page 20) and then give the assessments.

HANDOUT: Math Troubleshooter page. Go over the suggestions. Refer to these later as students do worksheets.

CLASSROOM DRILL: After students have practiced the basic facts for a few days, use some of the games given in earlier books. For example, Multiplication Match-up (page 30) or Divisor Racko (page 81) in the *Math Phonics*™*–Multiplication & Division Bonus Book.*

WORKSHEETS: Let students practice with pages 26-27 in class. List the facts that they do not know so that they can study those. Later, give the pages 26-27 as an assessment.

OPTIONAL: Run off copies of the basic facts page (page 20), and the *Math Phonics*™ rules pages (pages 21-25). Students can keep these in their math notebooks to study later. The math notebook can be a purchased three-hole pocket folder or made from a grocery sack. Instructions for the grocery sack folder can be found in the first six *Math Phonics*™ books (page 7).

Use materials for Math Skill of the Week (pages 26-28) in *Math Phonics*™*–Multiplication & Division Bonus Book.* Focus on the more difficult groups of multiplication and division facts.

WHY STUDENTS GET STUMPED

1. Working too fast.
2. Not reading the problem carefully.
3. Not writing down steps—doing too much in your head.
4. Not asking for help.
5. Not checking your answer.
6. Not looking for patterns.
7. Giving up before finishing the problem.
8. Not understanding the problem.
9. Using the wrong process.
10. Working without thinking.

WHAT TO DO WHEN YOU'RE STUMPED

1. Read the problem again.
2. Write down all the facts.
3. Start over on a new piece of paper.
4. Try another method.
5. Think of the problem in a new way.
6. Look at a sample problem.
7. Try a similar problem with smaller numbers.
8. Ask for help.
9. Go for a short walk.
10. Have a snack—protein is a great brain food.

SUBTRACTION FACTS

−0	−1	−2	−3	−4
0 − 0 = 0	1 − 1 = 0	2 − 2 = 0	3 − 3 = 0	4 − 4 = 0
1 − 0 = 1	2 − 1 = 1	3 − 2 = 1	4 − 3 = 1	5 − 4 = 1
2 − 0 = 2	3 − 1 = 2	4 − 2 = 2	5 − 3 = 2	6 − 4 = 2
3 − 0 = 3	4 − 1 = 3	5 − 2 = 3	6 − 3 = 3	7 − 4 = 3
4 − 0 = 4	5 − 1 = 4	6 − 2 = 4	7 − 3 = 4	8 − 4 = 4
5 − 0 = 5	6 − 1 = 5	7 − 2 = 5	8 − 3 = 5	9 − 4 = 5
6 − 0 = 6	7 − 1 = 6	8 − 2 = 6	9 − 3 = 6	10 − 4 = 6
7 − 0 = 7	8 − 1 = 7	9 − 2 = 7	10 − 3 = 7	11 − 4 = 7
8 − 0 = 8	9 − 1 = 8	10 − 2 = 8	11 − 3 = 8	12 − 4 = 8
9 − 0 = 9	10 − 1 = 9	11 − 2 = 9	12 − 3 = 9	13 − 4 = 9

−5	−6	−7	−8	−9
5 − 5 = 0	6 − 6 = 0	7 − 7 = 0	8 − 8 = 0	9 − 9 = 0
6 − 5 = 1	7 − 6 = 1	8 − 7 = 1	9 − 8 = 1	10 − 9 = 1
7 − 5 = 2	8 − 6 = 2	9 − 7 = 2	10 − 8 = 2	11 − 9 = 2
8 − 5 = 3	9 − 6 = 3	10 − 7 = 3	11 − 8 = 3	12 − 9 = 3
9 − 5 = 4	10 − 6 = 4	11 − 7 = 4	12 − 8 = 4	13 − 9 = 4
10 − 5 = 5	11 − 6 = 5	12 − 7 = 5	13 − 8 = 5	14 − 9 = 5
11 − 5 = 6	12 − 6 = 6	13 − 7 = 6	14 − 8 = 6	15 − 9 = 6
12 − 5 = 7	13 − 6 = 7	14 − 7 = 7	15 − 8 = 7	16 − 9 = 7
13 − 5 = 8	14 − 6 = 8	15 − 7 = 8	16 − 8 = 8	17 − 9 = 8
14 − 5 = 9	15 − 6 = 9	16 − 7 = 9	17 − 8 = 9	18 − 9 = 9

DIVISION FACTS

÷5	÷10	÷4	÷9	÷3	÷8
0 ÷ 5 = 0	0 ÷ 10 = 0	0 ÷ 4 = 0	0 ÷ 9 = 0	0 ÷ 3 = 0	0 ÷ 8 = 0
5 ÷ 5 = 1	10 ÷ 10 = 1	4 ÷ 4 = 1	9 ÷ 9 = 1	3 ÷ 3 = 1	8 ÷ 8 = 1
10 ÷ 5 = 2	20 ÷ 10 = 2	8 ÷ 4 = 2	18 ÷ 9 = 2	6 ÷ 3 = 2	16 ÷ 8 = 2
15 ÷ 5 = 3	30 ÷ 10 = 3	12 ÷ 4 = 3	27 ÷ 9 = 3	9 ÷ 3 = 3	24 ÷ 8 = 3
20 ÷ 5 = 4	40 ÷ 10 = 4	16 ÷ 4 = 4	36 ÷ 9 = 4	12 ÷ 3 = 4	32 ÷ 8 = 4
25 ÷ 5 = 5	50 ÷ 10 = 5	20 ÷ 4 = 5	45 ÷ 9 = 5	15 ÷ 3 = 5	40 ÷ 8 = 5
30 ÷ 5 = 6	60 ÷ 10 = 6	24 ÷ 4 = 6	54 ÷ 9 = 6	18 ÷ 3 = 6	48 ÷ 8 = 6
35 ÷ 5 = 7	70 ÷ 10 = 7	28 ÷ 4 = 7	63 ÷ 9 = 7	21 ÷ 3 = 7	56 ÷ 8 = 7
40 ÷ 5 = 8	80 ÷ 10 = 8	32 ÷ 4 = 8	72 ÷ 9 = 8	24 ÷ 3 = 8	64 ÷ 8 = 8
45 ÷ 5 = 9	90 ÷ 10 = 9	36 ÷ 4 = 9	81 ÷ 9 = 9	27 ÷ 3 = 9	72 ÷ 8 = 9
50 ÷ 5 = 10	100 ÷ 10 = 10	40 ÷ 4 = 10	90 ÷ 9 = 10	30 ÷ 3 = 10	80 ÷ 8 = 10

÷2	÷7	÷1	÷6
0 ÷ 2 = 0	0 ÷ 7 = 0	0 ÷ 1 = 0	0 ÷ 6 = 0
2 ÷ 2 = 1	7 ÷ 7 = 1	1 ÷ 1 = 1	6 ÷ 6 = 1
4 ÷ 2 = 2	14 ÷ 7 = 2	2 ÷ 1 = 2	12 ÷ 6 = 2
6 ÷ 2 = 3	21 ÷ 7 = 3	3 ÷ 1 = 3	18 ÷ 6 = 3
8 ÷ 2 = 4	28 ÷ 7 = 4	4 ÷ 1 = 4	24 ÷ 6 = 4
10 ÷ 2 = 5	35 ÷ 7 = 5	5 ÷ 1 = 5	30 ÷ 6 = 5
12 ÷ 2 = 6	42 ÷ 7 = 6	6 ÷ 1 = 6	36 ÷ 6 = 6
14 ÷ 2 = 7	49 ÷ 7 = 7	7 ÷ 1 = 7	42 ÷ 6 = 7
16 ÷ 2 = 8	56 ÷ 7 = 8	8 ÷ 1 = 8	48 ÷ 6 = 8
18 ÷ 2 = 9	63 ÷ 7 = 9	9 ÷ 1 = 9	54 ÷ 6 = 9
20 ÷ 2 = 10	70 ÷ 7 = 10	10 ÷ 1 = 10	60 ÷ 6 = 10

ADDITION FACTS

+0	+1	+2	+3	+4
0 + 0 = 0	1 + 0 = 1	2 + 0 = 2	3 + 0 = 3	4 + 0 = 4
0 + 1 = 1	1 + 1 = 2	2 + 1 = 3	3 + 1 = 4	4 + 1 = 5
0 + 2 = 2	1 + 2 = 3	2 + 2 = 4	3 + 2 = 5	4 + 2 = 6
0 + 3 = 3	1 + 3 = 4	2 + 3 = 5	3 + 3 = 6	4 + 3 = 7
0 + 4 = 4	1 + 4 = 5	2 + 4 = 6	3 + 4 = 7	4 + 4 = 8
0 + 5 = 5	1 + 5 = 6	2 + 5 = 7	3 + 5 = 8	4 + 5 = 9
0 + 6 = 6	1 + 6 = 7	2 + 6 = 8	3 + 6 = 9	4 + 6 = 10
0 + 7 = 7	1 + 7 = 8	2 + 7 = 9	3 + 7 = 10	4 + 7 = 11
0 + 8 = 8	1 + 8 = 9	2 + 8 = 10	3 + 8 = 11	4 + 8 = 12
0 + 9 = 9	1 + 9 = 10	2 + 9 = 11	3 + 9 = 12	4 + 9 = 13

+5	+6	+7	+8	+9
5 + 0 = 5	6 + 0 = 6	7 + 0 = 7	8 + 0 = 8	9 + 0 = 9
5 + 1 = 6	6 + 1 = 7	7 + 1 = 8	8 + 1 = 9	9 + 1 = 10
5 + 2 = 7	6 + 2 = 8	7 + 2 = 9	8 + 2 = 10	9 + 2 = 11
5 + 3 = 8	6 + 3 = 9	7 + 3 = 10	8 + 3 = 11	9 + 3 = 12
5 + 4 = 9	6 + 4 = 10	7 + 4 = 11	8 + 4 = 12	9 + 4 = 13
5 + 5 = 10	6 + 5 = 11	7 + 5 = 12	8 + 5 = 13	9 + 5 = 14
5 + 6 = 11	6 + 6 = 12	7 + 6 = 13	8 + 6 = 14	9 + 6 = 15
5 + 7 = 12	6 + 7 = 13	7 + 7 = 14	8 + 7 = 15	9 + 7 = 16
5 + 8 = 13	6 + 8 = 14	7 + 8 = 15	8 + 8 = 16	9 + 8 = 17
5 + 9 = 14	6 + 9 = 15	7 + 9 = 16	8 + 9 = 17	9 + 9 = 18

MULTIPLICATION FACTS

×5	×10	×4	×9	×3	×8
0 x 5 = 0	0 x 10 = 0	0 x 4 = 0	0 x 9 = 0	0 x 3 = 0	0 x 8 = 0
1 x 5 = 5	1 x 10 = 10	1 x 4 = 4	1 x 9 = 9	1 x 3 = 3	1 x 8 = 8
2 x 5 = 10	2 x 10 = 20	2 x 4 = 8	2 x 9 = 18	2 x 3 = 6	2 x 8 = 16
3 x 5 = 15	3 x 10 = 30	3 x 4 = 12	3 x 9 = 27	3 x 3 = 9	3 x 8 = 24
4 x 5 = 20	4 x 10 = 40	4 x 4 = 16	4 x 9 = 36	4 x 3 = 12	4 x 8 = 32
5 x 5 = 25	5 x 10 = 50	5 x 4 = 20	5 x 9 = 45	5 x 3 = 15	5 x 8 = 40
6 x 5 = 30	6 x 10 = 60	6 x 4 = 24	6 x 9 = 54	6 x 3 = 18	6 x 8 = 48
7 x 5 = 35	7 x 10 = 70	7 x 4 = 28	7 x 9 = 63	7 x 3 = 21	7 x 8 = 56
8 x 5 = 40	8 x 10 = 80	8 x 4 = 32	8 x 9 = 72	8 x 3 = 24	8 x 8 = 64
9 x 5 = 45	9 x 10 = 90	9 x 4 = 36	9 x 9 = 81	9 x 3 = 27	9 x 8 = 72
10 x 5 = 50	10 x 10 = 100	10 x 4 = 40	10 x 9 = 90	10 x 3 = 30	10 x 8 = 80

×2	×7	×1	×6
0 x 2 = 0	0 x 7 = 0	0 x 1 = 0	0 x 6 = 0
1 x 2 = 2	1 x 7 = 7	1 x 1 = 1	1 x 6 = 6
2 x 2 = 4	2 x 7 = 14	2 x 1 = 2	2 x 6 = 12
3 x 2 = 6	3 x 7 = 21	3 x 1 = 3	3 x 6 = 18
4 x 2 = 8	4 x 7 = 28	4 x 1 = 4	4 x 6 = 24
5 x 2 = 10	5 x 7 = 35	5 x 1 = 5	5 x 6 = 30
6 x 2 = 12	6 x 7 = 42	6 x 1 = 6	6 x 6 = 36
7 x 2 = 14	7 x 7 = 49	7 x 1 = 7	7 x 6 = 42
8 x 2 = 16	8 x 7 = 56	8 x 1 = 8	8 x 6 = 48
9 x 2 = 18	9 x 7 = 63	9 x 1 = 9	9 x 6 = 54
10 x 2 = 20	10 x 7 = 70	10 x 1 = 10	10 x 6 = 60

BASIC FACTS

EVEN NUMBERS CHANT

Two, four, six, eight, te-en, twelve,
Fo-ourteen, sixteen, eighteen, twenty.
Even numbers, they are fine!
Every other number on the number line.
Two, four, six, eight, te-en, twelve,
Fo-ourteen, sixteen, eighteen, twenty.
Even numbers, learn them best.
It'll be easy to learn the rest.

EVEN NUMBERS:

An even number is a number of students which can be put into two teams of the same size. Counting by 2s is a way of listing the even numbers.

ODD NUMBERS:

Any number ending in 1, 3, 5, 7 or 9 is an odd number.

DOUBLES:

Answers to doubles are always even numbers. Use 5 + 5 and 10 + 10 as foundation facts.

5 + 5 = 10–think of 5 fingers on each hand–10 in all. For 6 + 6, the answer is the next even number after 10. For 7 + 7, the answer is two even numbers after 10.

10 + 10 = 20–Just think of adding the 1s in the 10s column. For 9 + 9, the answer is 18, the even number just before 20. For 8 + 8, the answer is 16, the even number just before 18. Sums smaller than 10 do not need rules for most students.

NUMBER NEIGHBORS:

When adding number neighbors (two numbers side-by-side on the number line), double the smaller number and add 1. (Example: 5 + 6. Think: 5 + 5 = 10 so 5 + 6 is 11.)

Number neighbor answers are always odd numbers.

0s: When you add zero to a number, the number stays the same.

1s: When you add one to a number, the answer is the next number on the number line.

2s: When adding two to an even number, jump to the next even number. (6 + 2 = 8) When adding two to an odd number, jump to the next odd number. (9 + 2 = 11)

10s: When adding 10 to a one-digit number, just put a one in the 10s place. (4 + 10 = 14)

9s: To add nine to a number, add 10 and back up one. (4 + 9 Since 4 + 10 = 14, 4 + 9 = 13)

8s: To add eight to a number, add 10 and back up two. (4 + 8 Since 4 + 10 = 14, 4 + 8 = 12)

NUMBER PAIRS: To think of number pairs for any sum 11 through 18: (We will use 11 for our number.)
1. Use a ruler or number line.
2. Place index fingers on 1 and 10.
3. Draw an arc from the 1 to the 10.
4. Move index fingers one number towards the center.
5. Draw an arc from the 2 to the 9.
6. Continue until you reach 5 + 6. Write the number pairs.

$$1 + 10 = 11$$
$$2 + 9 = 11$$
$$3 + 8 = 11$$
$$4 + 7 = 11$$
$$5 + 6 = 11$$

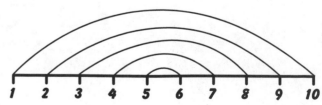

NUMBER NEIGHBORS: When you subtract a smaller number neighbor from a larger one, the answer is 1.

$$\begin{array}{r} 9 \\ -8 \\ \hline 1 \end{array}$$

When you subtract a larger number neighbor from a smaller one, the answer is 9.

$$\begin{array}{r} 18 \\ -9 \\ \hline 9 \end{array}$$

9 and 8 are number neighbors.

9s: When you subtract 9 from a teens number, subtract 10 and then add 1.

15 - 9 = ?

15 - 10 = 5 (spending $10)

15 - 9 = 6 (spending $9. You have more left.)

2s: When you subtract 2 from an even number, jump to the next smaller even number. (6 - 2 = 4)

When you subtract 2 from an odd number, jump to the next smaller odd number. (5 - 2 = 3)

0s: Any number times 0 equals 0.
($5 \times 0 = 0$)

1s: Any number times 1 equals that same number. ($6 \times 1 = 6$)

2s: Any number times 2 is that number added to itself–the same as the doubles for addition. ($5 \times 2 = 10$ and $5 + 5 = 10$)

4s: If you are stuck on 6×4, think $6 \times 2 = 12$. $12 + 12 = 24$. So $6 \times 4 = 24$.

5s: Five times an odd number ends in 5. ($5 \times 3 = 15$) Five times an even number ends in 0. ($5 \times 4 = 20$)

For five times an even number, take half of that even number and put it in the 10s place of the answer. Add a 0. ($5 \times 8 = 40$–4 is half of 8) It's like saying it takes two nickels to make each dime.

7s: The first four answers to the 7s are on a calendar–the 7 and the three numbers under it. (7, 14, 21 and 28)

$$7 \times 1 = 7$$
$$7 \times 2 = 14$$
$$7 \times 3 = 21$$
$$7 \times 4 = 28$$

9s: Nines answers are in pairs: 18 and 81, 27 and 72, 36 and 63, 45 and 54.

For answers 18 through 90, add the two digits. They equal 9.

$$1 + 8 = 9$$
$$2 + 7 = 9$$
$$3 + 6 = 9$$
$$4 + 5 = 9$$

If you are stuck on 9×6, remember the answer is in the 50s. We know $10 \times 6 = 60$ so 9×6 is less than 60–it is in the 50s. Since $5 + 4 = 9$, the answer is 54.

If you are stuck on 9×6 and can't remember the rule above, multiply 10×6 (10 groups of 6) and then subtract one group of 6.

$$9 \times 6 = ?$$

$10 \times 6 = 60$ (10 groups of 6)
$\underline{-6}$
54 (9 groups of 6)

10s: When multiplying a number by 10, add a 0 to the right of the number.

100s: When multiplying a number by 100, add two 0s to the right of the number.

MATH PHONICS™ RULES—DIVISION

2s: A number is divisible by 2 if it ends in 0, 2, 4, 6 or 8.

3s: A number is divisible by 3 if the sum of its digits is 3, 6 or 9. (15: 1 + 5 = 6 so 15 is divisible by 3.)

5s: A number is divisible by 5 if it ends in 5 or 0. (5, 10, 15 and 20 are all divisible by 5.

6s: A number is divisible by 6 if it is an even number and its digits add up to 3, 6 or 9. (18 is an even number and 1 + 8 = 9. So 18 is divisible by 6.)

9s: A number is divisible by 9 if the sum of its digits is divisible by 9. (3 + 6 = 9 so 36 is divisible by 9.) Sometimes you have to add more than once. (99: 9 + 9 = 18; 1 + 8 = 9 so 99 is divisible by 9.)

10s: A number is divisible by 10 if it ends in 0.

11s: A two-digit number is divisible by 11 if the two digits are the same. (44 is divisible by 11.) 44 ÷ 11 = 4

DIVIDING BY 10: Remove one zero or move the decimal point one place to the left.

DIVIDING BY 100: Remove two zeros or move the decimal point two places to the left.

Name _____

ADDITION & SUBTRACTION 11-18

1.
  6   5   7   9   6
 +6   +6   +9   +9   +7

2.
  8   6   4   7   9
 +6   +9   +7   +5   +5

3.
  7   8   5   3   8
 +8   +4   +8   +8   +8

4.
  9   8   4   7   2
 +3   +9   +9   +7   +9

5.
 14   15   11   12   13   11
 -5   -7   -2   -9   -5   -6

6.
 11   12   14   11   12   13
 -7   -6   -6   -3   -8   -4

7.
 13   11   12   14   11   12
 -9   -8   -5   -7   -4   -7

8.
 16   13   11   12   14   11
 -7   -8   -9   -4   -8   -5

9.
 14   15   13   16   12   15
 -9   -9   -7   -8   -3   -8

10.
 15   17   17   13   16   18
 -6   -8   -9   -6   -9   -9

MULTIPLICATION–3s-9s

1.	4 x4	5 x6	7 x7	3 x3	6 x6	8 x8	3 x9

1. 4   5   7   3   6   8   3
   x4   x6   x7   x3   x6   x8   x9

2. 3   5   4   4   3   6   5
   x6   x7   x5   x9   x4   x7   x9

3. 7   6   3   5   4   7   9
   x8   x8   x5   x5   x6   x9   x9

4. 4   3   5   6   8   3   4
   x8   x8   x8   x9   x9   x7   x7

DIVISION–3s-9s

5. 4)24   7)56   4)36   6)42   5)25   7)49   7)28   9)36

6. 7)42   3)18   8)64   9)72   5)20   7)35   9)45   6)24

7. 7)21   5)30   9)63   6)36   5)35   8)72   3)27   6)30

8. 3)24   4)16   8)40   8)32   6)54   3)12   8)48   9)27

9. 4)32   5)40   7)28   4)12   3)21   7)63   9)54   6)18

10. 3)15   5)15   8)56   6)48   9)81   4)20   8)24   5)45

LESSON PLAN 2: REVIEWING BASIC FRACTION SKILLS

OBJECTIVE: Review and assess students' basic fraction skills in order to build on those to teach new skills.

REVIEW: Survey the math facts which were missed on the assessments and have the class practice the more difficult groups for five minutes at the first of each class. For example, if the class needs practice adding 9s, they would chant:

1	+	9	=	10
2	+	9	=	11
3	+	9	=	12
4	+	9	=	13
5	+	9	=	14
6	+	9	=	15
7	+	9	=	16
8	+	9	=	17
9	+	9	=	18

Remind them of the rule for adding 9s—add 10 and then back up one. The next day, review another group and its rule. These could be featured as the Math Skill of the Week (pages 26-28) in *Math Phonics™—Multiplication & Division Bonus Book*.

MATERIALS: wall charts (pages 31-36), math notebooks, pages 63-82 in *Math Phonics™—Fractions* if needed, Cinco board game

DEMONSTRATION: Use the six pages of wall charts to review fraction skills. These charts are very basic. They present fraction concepts in slightly different ways than were taught in the *Math Phonics™—Fractions* book.

Make up other examples as needed. The illustrations on the Cinco gameboard (page 30) can be used as examples.

Review common denominators using the multiples strips (page 37) to help students remember multiples. Give each student a laminated page of strips and have them cut them into strips. Store them in a legal size envelope in the math folder. If student can't think of the common denominator for 5 and 12, get out those two strips and move the numbers until two match. 60 is the common denominator. See *Math Phonics™—Fractions*, page 85 for an explanation of finding least common denominators by finding prime factorizations.

Review multiplication of fractions using the fraction strips in the *Math Phonics™—Fractions* book. See Lesson Plan 8 (pages 73-75) for help in teaching that.

Review division of fractions. Use this example:

6 divided by $\frac{1}{3}$ means we need to find out how many thirds can be cut from 6 pizzas. Since there will be three cut from each pizza, we multiply by $\frac{3}{1}$ to find the answer to dividing by $\frac{1}{3}$. That's why we invert (flip over) the second fraction and multiply.

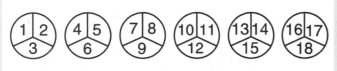

$$6 \div \frac{1}{3} = \frac{6}{1} \times \frac{3}{1} = \frac{18}{1} = 18$$

Here is a new way of teaching Changing Mixed Numbers to Improper Fractions. First, teach that $1 = \frac{1}{1}$.

$\frac{1}{2}$ means cut into two parts.

$\frac{1}{3}$ means cut into three parts.

$\frac{1}{1}$ means it hasn't been cut.

Then,

1. Write the whole number over 1.
$$3\frac{1}{5} = \frac{3}{1} + \frac{1}{5}$$

2. Change the denominator of the whole number.
$$\frac{3 \times 5}{1 \times 5} = \frac{15}{5}$$

3. Add.
$$\frac{15}{5} + \frac{1}{5} = \frac{16}{5}$$

If students understand the shorter way which was explained in *Math Phonics™– Fractions*, (page 69) don't make them use this method.

HANDOUT: The six wall charts may be copied and given to each student to keep in their math notebooks.

CLASSROOM DRILL–CINCO: If your students are just learning fractions, use the board game—Cinco. Use two regular dice. Run off a copy of the Cinco game for each student. Someone rolls the dice. Each number that is rolled can be used as a numerator or denominator for any of the fractions pictured. In the upper left-hand corner, there are five stars—one is shaded. The fraction is $\frac{1}{5}$. The two numbers from one wall may be used in two different boxes. The first person to get five complete fractions in a row as in bingo wins. Prizes may be gum candy, coupon for a day of free homework (coupons can be found in *Math Phonics™–Multiplication & Division Bonus Book*, page 27), or pencil, ruler, etc.

WORKSHEETS: Use the Fraction Review as a worksheet. Use pages from other *Math Phonics™* books if needed. After some review, give the Fraction Assessment. Determine what needs further practice.

OPTIONAL: Fraction Assessments in *Math Phonics™–Fractions* book, pages 90-91, can also be used as worksheets.

CINCO*

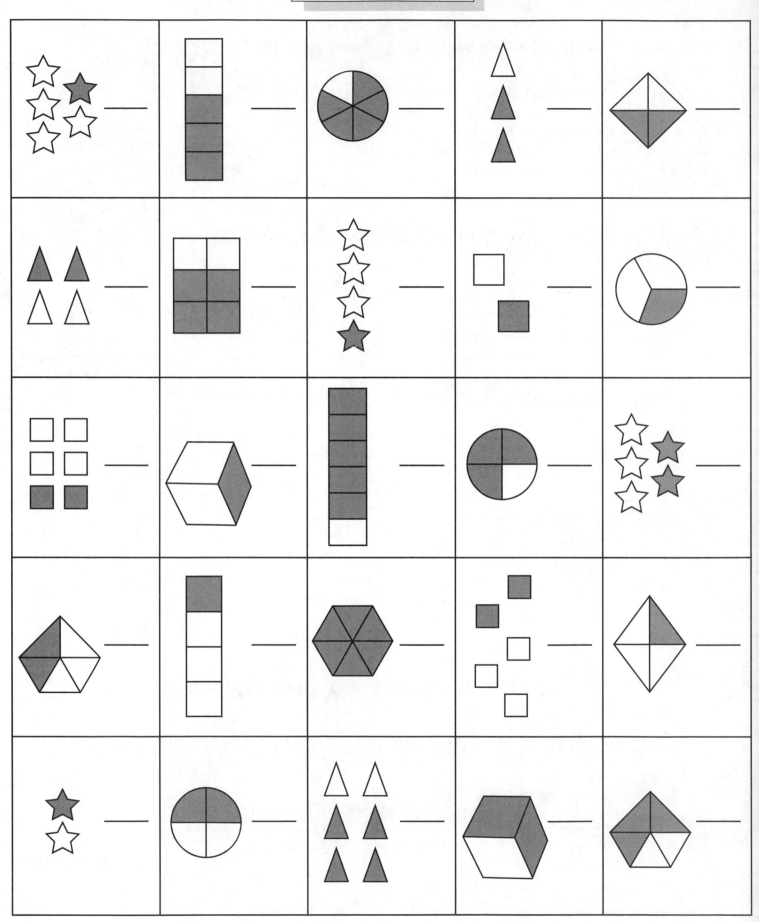

*Pronounced "Sink-o." Means "five" in Spanish.   TLC10347 Copyright © Teaching & Learning Company, Carthage, IL 62321-0010

FRACTION MEANS SOMETHING HAS BEEN DIVIDED.

$\dfrac{1}{4}$

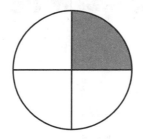

THINK OF A PIE—CUT INTO 4 PIECES.

$\dfrac{1}{4}$

WE ARE TALKING ABOUT ONE OF THE PIECES.

OR

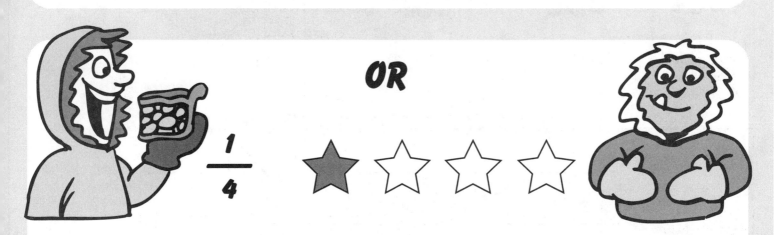

$\dfrac{1}{4}$

A GROUP OF OBJECTS HAS BEEN DIVIDED.

FOUR OBJECTS IN A GROUP—WE ARE TALKING ABOUT ONE OBJECT.

$\dfrac{1}{4}$ $\dfrac{\text{OBJECT WE ARE TALKING ABOUT}}{\text{TOTAL NUMBER OF OBJECTS}}$

ADDITION & SUBTRACTION OF FRACTIONS

DENOMINATORS* CAN BE THOUGHT OF AS LABELS!

$$\frac{1}{APPLE} + \frac{1}{APPLE} = \frac{2}{APPLES}$$

$$\frac{1}{3} + \frac{1}{3} = \frac{2}{3}$$

**ADD NUMBERS.
KEEP SAME LABEL.**

**ADD NUMERATORS.
KEEP SAME DENOMINATOR.**

SAME IDEA FOR SUBTRACTION

$$\frac{4}{5} - \frac{1}{5} = \frac{3}{5}$$

**SUBTRACT NUMERATORS.
KEEP SAME DENOMINATOR.**

*The denomination of paper money is its value—five-dollar bill, twenty-dollar bill, etc. The denomination of a church is its name or label.

$$\frac{1}{APPLE} + \frac{1}{PEACH} = \frac{2}{?}$$

What label should we use?

What do apples and peaches have in common?
Both are fruits.

If we can change both to the same label,

$$\frac{1}{FRUIT} + \frac{1}{FRUIT} = \frac{2}{FRUITS}$$

Then we can add.

WHAT DO TWO DENOMINATORS HAVE IN COMMON?

THE SAME MULTIPLE

$$\frac{1}{2} + \frac{1}{3} = ?$$

(Multiples of 2 are 2, 4, ⑥, 8, 10 . . .)
(Multiples of 3 are 3, ⑥, 9, 12, 15 . . .)
6 is the common multiple.

$$\begin{array}{r} \frac{1}{2} \times 3 = \frac{3}{6} \\ + \frac{1}{2} \times 2 = \frac{2}{6} \\ \hline \frac{5}{6} \end{array}$$

	$\frac{1}{2}$			$\frac{1}{3}$	
$\frac{1}{6}$	$\frac{1}{6}$	$\frac{1}{6}$	$\frac{1}{6}$	$\frac{1}{6}$	$\frac{1}{6}$

$$\frac{1}{2} + \frac{1}{3} = \frac{3}{6} + \frac{2}{6} = \frac{5}{6}$$

Changing to a larger denominator is like cutting the pie into more pieces.

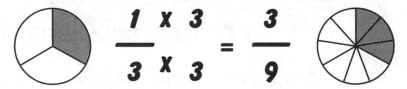

$$\frac{1 \times 3}{3 \times 3} = \frac{3}{9}$$

We are still talking about the same part of the pie, but
the numbers are larger and the pieces are smaller.

REDUCING IS THE OPPOSITE.

It talks about the same part of the pie using larger pieces and smaller numbers.

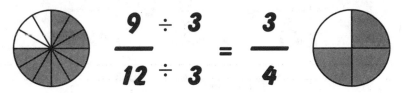

$$\frac{9 \div 3}{12 \div 3} = \frac{3}{4}$$

When you reduce, both parts of the fraction must be divisible by the same number.

RULES OF DIVISIBILITY

A number is divisible by:

2: If the number ends in 2, 4, 6, 8 or 0. (Example: 12, 38, 56, etc.)

3: If the digits add up to 3, 6 or 9. (Example: 2 + 1 = 3 so 21 is divisible by 3.)

5: If the number ends in 5 or 0. (Example: 10, 25, 40, etc.)

9: If the digits add up to 9. (Example: 3 + 6 = 9 so 36 is divisible by 9.)

10: If the number ends in 0. (Example: 10, 40, 70, etc.)

11: If a two-digit number has the same digit in the 10s place and 1s place.
(Example: 22, 33, 44 are all divisible by 11.)

$$\frac{1}{4} \times \frac{1}{3} = \frac{1}{12}$$ **(MULTIPLY NUMERATORS)**

(MULTIPLY DENOMINATORS)

$$\frac{1}{4} \times \frac{1}{3} \quad \textbf{MEANS} \quad \frac{1}{4} \textbf{ OF } \frac{1}{3}$$

Cut $\frac{1}{3}$ into four pieces.

| $\frac{1}{3}$ | $\frac{1}{3}$ | $\frac{1}{3}$ |

| $\frac{1}{12}$ | $\frac{1}{12}$ | $\frac{1}{12}$ | $\frac{1}{12}$ | $\frac{1}{12}$ | $\frac{1}{12}$ | $\frac{1}{12}$ | $\frac{1}{12}$ | $\frac{1}{12}$ | $\frac{1}{12}$ | $\frac{1}{12}$ | $\frac{1}{12}$ |

DIVISION OF FRACTIONS

REMEMBER THIS DIVISION RULE:

INVERT THE SECOND FRACTION AND MULTIPLY.

$3 \div \frac{1}{3}$ means

How many thirds can be cut from 3 pies? 9

Dividing by $\frac{1}{3}$ is the same as multiplying by $\frac{3}{1}$.

$$3 \div \frac{1}{3} = \frac{3}{1} \times \frac{3}{1} = \frac{9}{1} = 9$$

IMPROPER FRACTIONS

Improper fractions have the numerator larger than the denominator.

$$\frac{8}{4}$$

$\frac{8}{4}$ means 8 ÷ 4 or $4\overline{)\,\overset{2}{8}}$

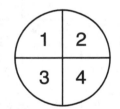

$$\frac{8}{4} = 2$$

$\frac{9}{4}$ means 9 ÷ 4 or $4\overline{)\,\overset{2\ r1}{9}}$ The remainder is a fraction.

$$\begin{array}{r} 8 \\ \hline 1 \end{array}$$

$$\frac{9}{4} = 2\frac{1}{4}$$

CHANGING A MIXED NUMBER TO AN IMPROPER FRACTION

1. Write the whole number over 1. $2\frac{1}{4} = \frac{2}{1} + \frac{1}{4}$

2. Change the denominator of the whole number. $\frac{2}{1} \times \frac{4}{4} = \frac{8}{4}$

3. Add the two fractions. $\frac{8}{4} + \frac{1}{4} = \frac{9}{4}$

2s –	2	4	6	8	10	12	14	16	18	20
3s –	3	6	9	12	15	18	21	24	27	30
4s –	4	8	12	16	20	24	28	32	36	40
5s –	5	10	15	20	25	30	35	40	45	50
6s –	6	12	18	24	30	36	42	48	54	60
7s –	7	14	21	28	35	42	49	56	63	70
8s –	8	16	24	32	40	48	56	64	72	80
9s –	9	18	27	36	45	54	63	72	81	90
10s –	10	20	30	40	50	60	70	80	90	
11s –	11	22	33	44	55	66	77	88	99	110
12s –	12	24	36	48	60	72	84	96	108	120

Name _____

FRACTION REVIEW

1. Reduce.

$$\frac{5 \div 5}{20 \div 5} = \qquad \frac{11}{33} = \qquad \frac{6}{15} = \qquad \frac{18}{27} = \qquad \frac{24}{36} =$$

2. Make equivalent fractions.

$$\frac{3 \times 4}{4 \times 4} = \frac{}{16} \qquad \frac{7}{10} = \frac{}{40} \qquad \frac{2}{3} = \frac{}{18} \qquad \frac{2}{7} = \frac{}{56} \qquad \frac{5}{9} = \frac{}{72}$$

3. Change to mixed numbers.

$$\frac{13}{4} = 3\frac{1}{4} \qquad \frac{10}{3} = \qquad \frac{15}{2} = \qquad \frac{22}{7} = \qquad \frac{13}{8} =$$

$$\begin{array}{r} 3\frac{1}{4} \\ 4\overline{)13} \\ \underline{12} \\ 1 \end{array}$$

4. Add or subtract. For answers, change all improper fractions to mixed numbers. Reduce answers if possible.

$$\begin{array}{r} \frac{1}{3} \\ + \ \frac{1}{3} \end{array} \qquad \frac{1}{2} \qquad \begin{array}{r} - \ \frac{1}{8} \\ \hline \end{array} \qquad \begin{array}{r} 12\frac{1}{7} \\ +13\frac{3}{14} \end{array} \qquad 13\frac{9}{10}$$

5. Change to improper fractions.

$$3\frac{1}{2} = \frac{7}{2} \qquad 2\frac{5}{8} = \qquad 5\frac{1}{4} = \qquad 6\frac{1}{3} =$$

$$\left(\frac{3}{1}+\frac{1}{2}\right) = \left(\frac{6}{2}+\frac{1}{2}=\frac{7}{2}\right) \text{ or } \left(\frac{3 \times 2}{1 \times 2}=\frac{6}{2}\right)$$

6. Multiply. Reduce if possible.

$$\frac{1}{3} \times \frac{1}{5} = \qquad \frac{3}{4} \times \frac{2}{10} = \qquad \frac{3}{8} \times \frac{2}{5} = \qquad \frac{2}{3} \times \frac{3}{10} =$$

7. Divide.

$$\frac{1}{2} \div \frac{1}{6} = \qquad \frac{3}{5} \div \frac{1}{5} = \qquad 1\frac{1}{3} \div \frac{1}{3} =$$

Name _____

FRACTION PRE-ASSESSMENT

1. Reduce.

$\frac{6}{10} =$ $\frac{3}{9} =$ $\frac{14}{21} =$ $\frac{35}{40} =$ $\frac{20}{50} =$

2. Make equivalent fractions.

$\frac{1}{2} = \frac{}{10}$ $\frac{3}{5} = \frac{}{15}$ $\frac{1}{4} = \frac{}{12}$ $\frac{7}{10} = \frac{}{80}$ $\frac{5}{8} = \frac{}{64}$

3. Change to mixed numbers.

$\frac{7}{4} =$ $\frac{11}{7} =$ $\frac{23}{12} =$ $\frac{19}{4} =$ $\frac{26}{11} =$

4. Change to improper fractions.

$2\frac{1}{3} =$ $2\frac{3}{4} =$ $5\frac{1}{3} =$ $5\frac{5}{6} =$ $7\frac{2}{5} =$

5. Add or subtract.

$\begin{array}{r} \frac{3}{4} \\ -\ \frac{1}{4} \end{array}$ $\begin{array}{r} \overline{} \\ \frac{1}{2} \end{array}$ $\begin{array}{r} +\ \frac{1}{4} \\ \overline{} \end{array}$ $\begin{array}{r} \frac{5}{8} \\ -\ \frac{1}{4} \end{array}$ $\begin{array}{r} \overline{} \\ \frac{7}{9} \end{array}$

6. Multiply.

$\frac{1}{2} \times \frac{1}{3} =$ $\frac{1}{4} \times \frac{2}{10} =$ $\frac{2}{3} \times \frac{4}{5} =$ $\frac{5}{6} \times \frac{6}{8} =$

7. Divide.

$\frac{1}{2} \div \frac{1}{8} =$ $\frac{2}{5} \div \frac{1}{5} =$ $1\frac{1}{4} \div \frac{1}{4} =$ $\frac{7}{10} \div \frac{1}{2} =$

LESSON PLAN 3
ADDITION & SUBTRACTION OF FRACTIONS WITH REGROUPING

OBJECTIVE: Build on students' knowledge of addition and subtraction of fractions. Teach regrouping from the whole numbers to the fractions and regrouping in answers.

REVIEW: Make sure students remember that they need a common denominator before adding or subtracting fractions. Review multiples using multiple strips if necessary. Review rules of divisibility (page 34) which can be used to make reducing easier.

DEMONSTRATION

1. Show some addition problems in which the answer contains a whole number and an improper fraction.

$$5\frac{1}{2} = \frac{2}{4}$$
$$+\,6\frac{3}{4} = \frac{3}{4}$$
$$\overline{\rule{0pt}{1em}11 \quad \frac{5}{4}}$$

$$11\frac{5}{4} = 11 + 1\frac{1}{4} = 12\frac{1}{4}$$

$$\left(\frac{5}{4} = 4\overline{)5}^{\,1\;\frac{1}{4}}\right)$$

2. Now practice with subtraction problems in which the minuend (top) fraction is smaller than the subtractor (lower) fraction.

$$17\frac{1}{3} = \frac{4}{12}$$
$$-\,9\frac{3}{4} = \frac{9}{12}$$

3. You must borrow 1 from the 17. Write it as $\frac{12}{12}$ to add to the $\frac{4}{12}$.

$$\overset{16}{\cancel{17}}\frac{1}{3} = \frac{4}{12} + \frac{12}{12} = \frac{16}{12}$$
$$-\,9\frac{3}{4} = \frac{9}{12} \quad = \quad \frac{9}{12} \quad = 7\frac{7}{12}$$
$$\overline{\rule{0pt}{1em}7} \qquad\qquad \frac{7}{12}$$

4. Next, explain subtraction problems in which the subtractor (lower) number does not have a fraction part.

$$10\frac{1}{3}$$
$$-\,7$$
$$\overline{\rule{0pt}{1em}3\frac{1}{3}}$$

There is nothing to subtract from the $\frac{1}{3}$. Just bring it down.

Also, explain subtraction problems in which the minuend has no fraction part.

$$15\frac{3}{3}$$
$$-\,6\frac{1}{3}$$
$$\overline{\rule{0pt}{1em}8\frac{2}{3}}$$

Borrow (regroup) $\frac{3}{3}$ from the 15.

HANDOUT: Divisibility Grid (page 45). You or the students can put in numbers at the left side to practice the rules of divisibility.

CLASSROOM DRILL: Give the class several sample problems for practice. Go through them step by step if necessary.

$$3\frac{2}{3} = \frac{10}{15}$$
$$+ 2\frac{4}{5} = \frac{12}{15}$$
$$\overline{5 \qquad \frac{22}{15}}$$

$$\frac{22}{15} = 15\overline{)22} = 1\frac{7}{15}$$

$$5 + 1\frac{7}{15} = 6\frac{7}{15}$$

Other samples:

$$6\frac{1}{2}$$
$$+ 5\frac{6}{7}$$

$$8\frac{3}{4}$$
$$- 2\frac{9}{10}$$

$$3\frac{2}{3}$$
$$+2\frac{4}{5}$$

WORKSHEETS: Pages 43 and 44 are self-explanatory. Use pages 46-49 as extra practice if necessary.

OPTIONAL: Page 42 has 78 problems but it should go fast. The reducing and equivalent fraction problems can be done right in each square. Tell students to use scratch paper for the mixed number and improper fraction problems if needed. Do the first two rows in class to give students a head start.

Word problems and activity pages will be focused on Alaska. Students may pretend they are taking a trip to Alaska.

Reducing to lowest terms means reducing and making sure there are no improper fractions in the answer.

Name _____

ALASKA!

$1\frac{1}{5}=\frac{6}{5}$	$\frac{10}{15}=\frac{2}{3}$	$\frac{9}{10}=\frac{63}{70}$	$\frac{7}{8}=\frac{28}{32}$	$\frac{6}{7}=\frac{36}{42}$	$\frac{5}{6}=\frac{30}{36}$
$1\frac{1}{8}=\frac{9}{8}$	$2\frac{1}{2}=\frac{6}{2}$	$3\frac{1}{4}=\frac{13}{4}$	$1\frac{5}{6}=\frac{10}{6}$	$1\frac{7}{8}=\frac{14}{8}$	$2\frac{1}{3}=\frac{8}{3}$
$\frac{3}{4}=\frac{12}{16}$	$\frac{3}{5}=\frac{9}{15}$	$\frac{1}{2}=\frac{11}{22}$	$\frac{9}{10}=\frac{98}{100}$	$\frac{7}{10}=\frac{77}{100}$	$1\frac{1}{3}=\frac{5}{3}$
$\frac{10}{9}=1\frac{2}{9}$	$\frac{1}{4}=\frac{5}{16}$	$\frac{1}{9}=\frac{2}{27}$	$\frac{1}{11}=\frac{33}{44}$	$\frac{13}{12}=1\frac{1}{10}$	$\frac{15}{14}=1\frac{1}{15}$
$\frac{9}{18}=\frac{1}{2}$	$\frac{50}{100}=\frac{1}{3}$	$\frac{75}{100}=\frac{1}{2}$	$\frac{1}{3}=\frac{11}{33}$	$\frac{1}{7}=\frac{4}{28}$	$\frac{15}{7}=2\frac{1}{7}$
$\frac{300}{400}=\frac{3}{4}$	$\frac{12}{7}=1\frac{3}{7}$	$\frac{7}{21}=\frac{1}{4}$	$\frac{2}{22}=\frac{1}{11}$	$\frac{8}{32}=\frac{1}{3}$	$\frac{1}{2}=\frac{33}{66}$
$\frac{21}{10}=2\frac{1}{10}$	$\frac{18}{27}=\frac{2}{3}$	$\frac{55}{66}=\frac{5}{6}$	$\frac{77}{88}=\frac{7}{8}$	$\frac{9}{5}=1\frac{3}{5}$	$\frac{11}{10}=1\frac{1}{10}$
$\frac{9}{7}=1\frac{1}{7}$	$\frac{25}{40}=\frac{7}{8}$	$\frac{11}{8}=1\frac{1}{8}$	$\frac{10}{20}=\frac{1}{3}$	$\frac{1}{3}=\frac{3}{12}$	$\frac{1}{4}=\frac{4}{12}$
$\frac{6}{5}=1\frac{1}{5}$	$\frac{10}{12}=\frac{5}{6}$	$\frac{15}{18}=\frac{5}{6}$	$\frac{11}{44}=\frac{1}{4}$	$\frac{100}{200}=\frac{1}{2}$	$\frac{8}{7}=1\frac{1}{7}$
$\frac{3}{15}=\frac{1}{5}$	$\frac{6}{15}=\frac{1}{5}$	$\frac{9}{15}=\frac{3}{5}$	$\frac{4}{16}=\frac{1}{3}$	$\frac{15}{20}=\frac{2}{3}$	$\frac{7}{5}=1\frac{3}{5}$
$\frac{11}{33}=\frac{1}{3}$	$\frac{20}{50}=\frac{2}{5}$	$\frac{22}{55}=\frac{2}{5}$	$\frac{4}{2}=1\frac{1}{2}$	$\frac{90}{100}=\frac{4}{5}$	$\frac{8}{12}=\frac{1}{2}$
$\frac{3}{12}=\frac{1}{3}$	$\frac{2}{6}=\frac{1}{7}$	$\frac{3}{2}=2\frac{1}{2}$	$\frac{4}{10}=\frac{1}{5}$	$\frac{7}{3}=2\frac{1}{2}$	$3\frac{2}{2}=5$
$\frac{1}{3}=\frac{2}{6}$	$\frac{3}{4}=\frac{9}{12}$	$\frac{6}{5}=1\frac{1}{5}$	$\frac{7}{14}=\frac{1}{2}$	$\frac{10}{30}=\frac{1}{3}$	$\frac{5}{15}=\frac{1}{3}$

Shade or color all the correct equivalent fractions to answer this question: When did Alaska become a state? _____ Hold the page this way to read the answer. Use fraction circles or fraction strips if you need help.

DIVISIBILITY

Write *yes* or *no* in each section of the grid to show if the numbers at the left are divisible by each number at the top.

RULES OF DIVISIBILITY

1. Divisible by 2: if it ends in 0, 2, 4, 6 or 8.
2. Divisible by 5: if it ends in 0 or 5.
3. Divisible by 9: if the digits add up to 9.
4. Divisible by 10: if it ends in 0.

NUMBER	DIVISIBLE BY ?			
	2	5	9	10
20				
36				
15				
18				
30				
45				
72				

Reduce. Use rules of divisibility.

1. $\dfrac{6}{10} =$ $\dfrac{15}{25} =$ $\dfrac{10}{30} =$ $\dfrac{27}{36} =$ $\dfrac{25}{45} =$

Rename these mixed numbers so that the fraction is a proper fraction.

2. $2\frac{3}{3} = 2 + 1 = 3$ $4\frac{6}{5} = (4 + 1\frac{1}{5} = 5\frac{1}{5})$ $5\frac{7}{6} =$ $10\frac{9}{7} =$

   $(\frac{6}{5} = 1\frac{1}{5})$

3. $4\frac{11}{5} =$ $9\frac{12}{7} =$ $6\frac{11}{3} =$ $18\frac{11}{9} =$

4. Your visit to Alaska has just begun! You have crossed the Canada-Alaska border on the Alaska Highway. The driver says you will stop for the night in $3\frac{7}{4}$ hours. Rewrite the number without the improper fraction. _____

5. The guide book says in Barrow, Alaska, (the northernmost settlement in Alaska) the sun does not rise above the horizon for about 50 days each year. What fraction of a year is that? Reduce to lowest terms. _____

CHALLENGE:
Solve this to see the number of square miles in Alaska. The digit in the ten thousands place is double the digit in the hundreds place. The digit in the hundred thousands place is one less than the digit in the thousands place (which is two more than the digit in the hundreds). The rest are zeros.

___ ___ ___, _4_ ___ ___ square miles

DIVISIBILITY

Write *yes* or *no* in each section of the grid to show if the numbers at the left are divisible by each number at the top.

RULES OF DIVISIBILITY

1. Divisible by 3: if the digits add up to 3, 6 or 9.

2. Divisible by 5: if it ends in 0 or 5.

3. Divisible by 9: if the digits add up to 9. (Sometimes you have to add more than once.)

4. Divisible by 11: for a two-digit number, it has the same digit in the 10s and 1s place.

	DIVISIBLE BY ?			
NUMBER	3	5	9	11
30				
63				
45				
55				
99				
144				
33				

Add. Change all improper fractions in answers to mixed numbers. Reduce answers to lowest terms.

1. $6\frac{1}{5}$ _____ $+ 7\frac{5}{9}$ $9\frac{1}{2}$

   $+ 5\frac{2}{5}$ $8\frac{2}{9}$ $+ 7\frac{1}{5}$

2. $8\frac{5}{6}$ _____ $+ 6\frac{4}{5}$ $5\frac{5}{6}$

   $+ 3\frac{1}{2}$ $7\frac{2}{3}$ $+ 9\frac{3}{4}$

3. Alaska is nearly $\frac{110}{550}$ as large as the 48 continental states. Reduce the fraction. _____

4. The guide book says the Denali National Park Safaris last $\frac{63}{18}$ hours. Reduce and simplify the fraction, changing to a mixed number. _____

CHALLENGE:

Add these numbers to find the year Captain Barnette founded a trading post where Fairbanks now stands.

$$880 + 929.33 + 70.73 + 20.94 = \underline{\quad\quad}$$

DIVISIBILITY GRID

Write *yes* or *no* in each section of the grid to show if the numbers at the left are divisible by each number at the top.

NUMBER	DIVISIBLE BY					
	2	3	5	9	10	11

A number is divisible by:

2 if it ends in 0, _____, _____, _____ or _____.

3 if the sum of its digits is 3, _____ or _____.

5 if it ends in _____ or _____.

9 if the sum of its digits is _____. (Sometimes you have to add more than once.)

11 if it is a two-digit number and the two digits are _____ _____.

Note: These rules of divisibility are easy to remember. Remind students to think of these when reducing.

CHANGING MIXED NUMBERS TO IMPROPER FRACTIONS

1. $4\frac{1}{5} = (\frac{4}{1} + \frac{1}{5}) = (\frac{20}{5} + \frac{1}{5} = \frac{21}{5})$ $3\frac{1}{4} =$

    $(\frac{4 \times 5}{1 \times 5} = \frac{20}{5})$

2. $5\frac{1}{2} =$ $7\frac{1}{3} =$

3. $8\frac{3}{5} =$ $6\frac{5}{9} =$

REVIEW REDUCING.

4. $\frac{14}{18} =$ $\frac{15}{25} =$ $\frac{12}{18} =$ $\frac{18}{27} =$

5. $\frac{10}{40} =$ $\frac{30}{45} =$ $\frac{24}{30} =$ $\frac{14}{28} =$

EQUIVALENT FRACTIONS

6. $\frac{3}{5} = \frac{}{25}$ $\frac{9}{10} = \frac{}{40}$ $\frac{8}{11} = \frac{}{44}$ $\frac{6}{7} = \frac{}{35}$

7. $\frac{5}{8} = \frac{}{64}$ $\frac{7}{8} = \frac{}{40}$ $\frac{5}{6} = \frac{}{24}$ $\frac{7}{10} = \frac{}{100}$

8. $\frac{6}{9} = \frac{}{72}$ $\frac{3}{4} = \frac{}{100}$ $\frac{1}{4} = \frac{}{36}$ $\frac{2}{3} = \frac{}{33}$

ADDITION OF FRACTIONS WITH REGROUPING

Add. Reduce.

1. $6\frac{1}{3}$ $3\frac{1}{5}$ $10\frac{1}{7}$ $12\frac{1}{3}$
   $+\,4\frac{1}{3}$ $+\,2\frac{2}{5}$ $+\,6\frac{2}{7}$ $+\,4\frac{1}{3}$

2. $3\frac{1}{4}$ $2\frac{1}{2}$ $5\frac{1}{3}$ $9\frac{1}{4}$
   $+\,6\frac{1}{3}$ $+\,5\frac{1}{5}$ $+\,6\frac{1}{5}$ $+\,8\frac{1}{5}$

3. $2\frac{2}{3}$ $3\frac{4}{5}$ $6\frac{2}{3}$ $8\frac{9}{10}$
   $+\,1\frac{3}{4}$ $+\,5\frac{1}{2}$ $+\,3\frac{7}{8}$ $+\,7\frac{4}{5}$

4. $10\frac{2}{3}$ $12\frac{7}{8}$ $15\frac{7}{10}$ $12\frac{5}{8}$
   $+\,7\frac{4}{5}$ $+\,9\frac{2}{3}$ $+\,6\frac{3}{4}$ $+\,7\frac{6}{7}$

SUBTRACTION OF FRACTIONS WITH REGROUPING

Subtract. Reduce.

1.
$\quad 3$
$-\ 1\frac{1}{2}$

$\quad 5$
$-\ 2\frac{1}{3}$

$\quad 6$
$-\ 1\frac{2}{5}$

$\quad 8$
$-\ 3\frac{3}{7}$

$\quad 10$
$-\ 5\frac{5}{8}$

2.
$\quad 3\frac{3}{4}$
$-\ 1\frac{1}{3}$

$\quad 4\frac{5}{6}$
$-\ 2\frac{1}{2}$

$\quad 7\frac{9}{10}$
$-\ 3$

$\quad 8\frac{7}{12}$
$-\ 4\frac{1}{3}$

$\quad 9\frac{3}{5}$
$-\ 4\frac{1}{2}$

3.
$\quad 4\frac{1}{2}$
$-\ 2\frac{3}{4}$

$\quad 6\frac{1}{3}$
$-\ 1$

$\quad 9\frac{1}{4}$
$-\ 3\frac{2}{5}$

$\quad 8\frac{1}{7}$
$-\ 2\frac{2}{3}$

$\quad 10\frac{1}{5}$
$-\ 3\frac{2}{3}$

4.
$\quad 5\frac{1}{7}$
$-\ 1$

$\quad 21\frac{1}{2}$
$-\ 7\frac{3}{5}$

$\quad 18\frac{1}{3}$
$-11\frac{4}{7}$

$\quad 25\frac{1}{5}$
$-17\frac{2}{3}$

$\quad 27\frac{1}{9}$
$-\ 8\frac{3}{7}$

5.
$\quad 12\frac{1}{4}$
$-\ 7\frac{1}{3}$

$\quad 16\frac{2}{5}$
$-\ 7\frac{2}{3}$

$\quad 21\frac{1}{10}$
-13

$\quad 18\frac{1}{6}$
$-13\frac{3}{5}$

$\quad 29\frac{2}{3}$
$-18\frac{11}{12}$

ADDITION & SUBTRACTION OF MIXED NUMBERS

1. $6\frac{1}{5}$ $\quad\quad\quad$ $4\frac{1}{3}$ $\quad\quad\quad$ $10\frac{2}{7}$ $\quad\quad\quad$ $8\frac{2}{9}$
    $+5\frac{2}{5}$ $\quad\quad$ $+5\frac{1}{3}$ $\quad\quad$ $+9\frac{3}{7}$ $\quad\quad$ $+6\frac{5}{9}$

2. $2\frac{1}{3}$ $\quad\quad\quad$ $5\frac{1}{2}$ $\quad\quad\quad$ $8\frac{1}{3}$ $\quad\quad\quad$ $10\frac{1}{4}$
    $+3\frac{1}{4}$ $\quad\quad$ $+6\frac{1}{5}$ $\quad\quad$ $+7\frac{1}{5}$ $\quad\quad$ $+9\frac{1}{5}$

3. $5\frac{3}{5}$ $\quad\quad\quad$ $6\frac{5}{7}$ $\quad\quad\quad$ $9\frac{8}{9}$ $\quad\quad\quad$ 12
    $-2\frac{1}{5}$ $\quad\quad$ $-3\frac{2}{7}$ $\quad\quad$ $-3\frac{4}{9}$ $\quad\quad$ $-9\frac{4}{6}$

4. $7\frac{3}{4}$ $\quad\quad\quad$ $8\frac{5}{6}$ $\quad\quad\quad$ $11\frac{7}{12}$ $\quad\quad\quad$ $12\frac{4}{5}$
    -2 $\quad\quad\quad$ $-3\frac{1}{2}$ $\quad\quad$ $-4\frac{1}{4}$ $\quad\quad$ $-9\frac{1}{2}$

Reduce.

5. $\frac{5}{10}=$ $\quad\quad\quad$ $\frac{9}{12}=$ $\quad\quad\quad$ $\frac{7}{14}=$ $\quad\quad\quad$ $\frac{15}{20}=$ $\quad\quad\quad$ $\frac{16}{24}=$

Change to a mixed number. Reduce.

6. $\frac{15}{10}=$ $\quad\quad\quad\quad$ $\frac{21}{12}=$ $\quad\quad\quad\quad$ $\frac{30}{25}=$

7. $\frac{42}{35}=$ $\quad\quad\quad\quad$ $\frac{12}{7}=$ $\quad\quad\quad\quad$ $\frac{20}{15}=$

OBJECTIVE: Explain cancelling within a problem before multiplying; teach multiplying and dividing mixed numbers.

REVIEW

1. Once again, go over changing mixed numbers to improper fractions. Show the shortcut. Tell them to continue using the longer method if it makes more sense to them.

   Longer Method: $3\frac{1}{2} = (\frac{3}{1} + \frac{1}{2})$ $\frac{3 \times 2}{1 \times 2} = \frac{6}{2}$ $(\frac{6}{2} + \frac{1}{2} = \frac{7}{2})$

   Shorter Method: $3\frac{1}{2} = \frac{7}{2}$ $(2 \times 3 = 6; 6 + 1 = 7)$

2. Review the Rules of Divisibility (page 34) to help with cancelling. Cancelling is reducing before multiplying the fractions.

DEMONSTRATION
Cancelling
In this problem

$$\frac{2}{3} \times \frac{3}{4} = \frac{6}{12}$$

The answer can be reduced by dividing both numbers by 6.

$$\frac{6 \div 6}{12 \div 6} = \frac{1}{2}$$

Look at the problem in a different way.

$$\frac{2}{3} \times \frac{3}{4} = \frac{2 \times 3}{3 \times 4}$$

There is a factor of 3 in the numerator and denominator. Divide each three by 3 leaving a 1 in each place. This is like reducing before you multiply.

$$\frac{2 \times \overset{1}{\cancel{3}}}{\cancel{3} \times 4}$$
$$\scriptstyle 1$$

The 2 and the 4 are both divisible by 2.

$$\frac{\overset{1}{\cancel{2}} \times \overset{1}{\cancel{3}}}{\underset{1}{\cancel{3}} \times \underset{2}{\cancel{4}}}$$

Now multiply.

$$\frac{\overset{1}{\cancel{2}} \times \overset{1}{\cancel{3}}}{\underset{1}{\cancel{3}} \times \underset{2}{\cancel{4}}} = \frac{1}{2}$$

This is the same answer we got by multiplying and reducing.

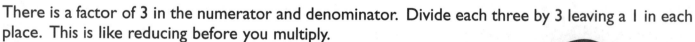

$$\frac{2}{3} \times \frac{3}{4} = \frac{6 \div 6}{12 \div 6} = \frac{1}{2}$$

WEIGHT REDUCTION PLAN

MIXED NUMBERS: If your problem has a mixed number, change it to an improper fraction and then multiply.

$$1\frac{1}{2} \times \frac{3}{4} =$$

$$\frac{3}{2} \times \frac{3}{4} = \frac{9}{8} = 1\frac{1}{8}$$

$$8\overline{)9} \quad \frac{1\frac{1}{8}}{\frac{8}{1}}$$

For division with mixed numbers, change the mixed numbers to improper fractions and then divide (flip over the second fraction and multiply).

$$2\frac{1}{2} \div \frac{1}{2} =$$

$$\frac{5}{2} \times \frac{2}{1} =$$

When you are ready to multiply, see if anything can be cancelled.

$$\frac{5}{\underset{1}{\cancel{2}}} \times \frac{\cancel{2}^{1}}{1} = \frac{5}{1} = 5$$

This make sense:

$2\frac{1}{2} \div \frac{1}{2}$ means how many half pizzas can be made from $2\frac{1}{2}$ pizzas.

The answer is 5.

HANDOUT: The worksheet for page 52 can be used in class for practice in cancelling.

CLASSROOM DRILL: One student can do a problem from page 52 at the board while the other students work at their desks. Notice that the two top groups of problems are the same.

For the word problems, if they talk about $\frac{3}{4}$ of something, *of* means "times." You will multiply fractions.

WORKSHEETS: Remind students that when multiplying or dividing using whole numbers and fractions (page 56), they must put the whole number over 1.

$$\frac{4}{5} \times 20 =$$

$$\frac{4}{5} \times \frac{20}{1} =$$

OPTIONAL: Pages 56 and 57 are extra practice pages if needed.

CANCELLING

Multiply. Then reduce.

1. $\dfrac{1}{2}$ x $\dfrac{2}{3}$ = $\dfrac{3}{4}$ x $\dfrac{1}{3}$ = $\dfrac{2}{3}$ x $\dfrac{6}{10}$ =

2. $\dfrac{1}{2}$ x $\dfrac{4}{9}$ = $\dfrac{9}{10}$ x $\dfrac{2}{3}$ = $\dfrac{1}{3}$ x $\dfrac{9}{10}$ =

Cancel. Then multiply.

3. $\dfrac{1}{2}$ x $\dfrac{2}{3}$ = $\dfrac{3}{4}$ x $\dfrac{1}{3}$ = $\dfrac{2}{3}$ x $\dfrac{6}{10}$ =

4. $\dfrac{1}{2}$ x $\dfrac{4}{9}$ = $\dfrac{9}{10}$ x $\dfrac{2}{3}$ = $\dfrac{1}{3}$ x $\dfrac{9}{10}$ =

Add or subtract. Reduce to lowest terms.

5. $32\frac{1}{2}$ _____ $+59\frac{3}{4}$
     $+29\frac{1}{5}$ $47\frac{2}{3}$

6. Your family has $2\frac{1}{3}$ more hours of driving and then $1\frac{1}{4}$ hours to rest before meeting up with the wildlife cruise. What is the total number of hours before the cruise? _____

7. You have reservations for next Saturday to cruise Prince William Sound aboard the *Klondike Express*. The travel brochure says $\frac{3}{4}$ of the cruise guests usually see whales and $\frac{1}{2}$ of the $\frac{3}{4}$ also see seals. What fraction of the guests see the seals? _____

CHALLENGE:

Complete these problems and put each letter in the blank space corresponding to the answer. Find out what the Aleut tribe called this northern state.

$\frac{5}{6}$ x $\frac{2}{5}$ =	$\frac{9}{10}$ x $\frac{5}{3}$ =	$\frac{1}{2}$ x $\frac{8}{9}$ =	$\frac{1}{3}$ x $\frac{6}{7}$ =	$\frac{3}{8}$ x $\frac{1}{3}$ =	$\frac{7}{8}$ x $\frac{4}{5}$ =
E	**S**	**L**	**Y**	**A**	**K**

$\dfrac{1}{8}$ $\dfrac{4}{9}$ $\dfrac{2}{7}$ $\dfrac{1}{3}$ $1\frac{1}{2}$ $\dfrac{7}{10}$ $\dfrac{1}{8}$

MULTIPLYING IMPROPER FRACTIONS

1. $1\frac{1}{2} \times \frac{1}{3} =$ $1\frac{1}{3} \times 2 =$ $3\frac{1}{4} \times 4 =$

2. $1\frac{1}{4} \times 1\frac{1}{3} =$ $2\frac{1}{2} \times \frac{1}{5} =$ $3\frac{1}{3} \times \frac{6}{10} =$

Cancel. Then multiply.

3. $\frac{7}{8} \times \frac{4}{5} =$ $\frac{5}{6} \times \frac{3}{10} =$ $\frac{7}{12} \times \frac{4}{14} =$

Reduce answers to lowest terms.

4. $12\frac{7}{8}$ $-18\frac{1}{5}$
            $+9\frac{2}{3}$ $35\frac{1}{7}$

5. Your itinerary calls for a $2\frac{4}{5}$-hour ride on a float plane. It says $\frac{2}{7}$ of that time you will be travelling through iceberg-packed waters. How many hours will you be amidst icebergs? _____

6. While in Anchorage, you have been told to visit the Imaginarium. Of your $3\frac{1}{5}$ hours there, $\frac{3}{4}$ of the time will be in the planetarium. How long will you be in the planetarium? _____

CHALLENGE:
Solve these problems and fill in the blanks to learn the term for a piece breaking off of an iceberg.

$2\frac{1}{4} \times \frac{2}{3} =$	$5\frac{1}{3} \times \frac{3}{4} =$	$2\frac{1}{6} \times \frac{3}{4} =$	$5\frac{1}{7} \times \frac{7}{12} =$	$5\frac{3}{5} \times \frac{2}{7} =$	$4\frac{1}{2} \times 1\frac{2}{3} =$	$4\frac{1}{6} \times \frac{2}{5} =$
L	**I**	**G**	**C**	**V**	**N**	**A**

$\overline{}\ \overline{}\ \overline{}\ \overline{}\ \overline{}\ \overline{}\ \overline{}$
3    $1\frac{2}{3}$ $1\frac{1}{2}$ $1\frac{3}{5}$ 4 $7\frac{1}{2}$ $1\frac{5}{8}$

Name _____   WORKSHEET K

DIVISION OF FRACTIONS

Change to improper fractions and divide.

1. $1\frac{1}{2} \div \frac{1}{4} =$ $\qquad$ $2\frac{1}{3} \div 1\frac{1}{6} =$

2. $3\frac{2}{3} \div 1\frac{1}{3} =$ $\qquad$ $3\frac{3}{4} \div \frac{3}{4} =$

Reduce answers to lowest terms.

3. $4\frac{1}{8} \times 5\frac{1}{3} =$ $\qquad$ $2\frac{2}{7} \times 2\frac{7}{8} =$ $\qquad$ $6\frac{3}{7} \times 4\frac{1}{5} =$

Reduce answers to lowest terms.

4. $\quad 24\frac{3}{4}$ $\qquad$ $\underline{\qquad}$ $\qquad$ $+38\frac{3}{8}$
    $\quad -16\frac{1}{3}$ $\qquad$ $59\frac{1}{16}$

5. $\quad 43\frac{5}{12}$ $\qquad$ $\underline{\qquad}$ $\qquad$ $+86\frac{3}{5}$
    $\quad +79\frac{7}{8}$ $\qquad$ $27\frac{3}{4}$

Change to improper fractions.

6. $10\frac{1}{2} =$ $\qquad$ $7\frac{1}{8} =$ $\qquad$ $16\frac{1}{3} =$

7. $5\frac{4}{9} =$ $\qquad$ $11\frac{3}{4} =$ $\qquad$ $13\frac{5}{9} =$

TLC10347 Copyright © Teaching & Learning Company, Carthage, IL 62321-0010

SNOWMAN MATH

Do each problem and draw a line to the correct answer. Reduce!

$\frac{4}{5}$ X $\frac{15}{16}$ =

$10\frac{1}{5}$

$2\frac{1}{4}$

$\frac{11}{12}$ ÷ $\frac{5}{6}$ =

$\frac{3}{4}$

$5\frac{1}{4}$ X $\frac{2}{9}$ =

$1\frac{1}{10}$

$1\frac{1}{6}$

$1\frac{1}{6}$ ÷ $2\frac{11}{12}$ =

$\frac{3}{4}$ ÷ $4\frac{1}{8}$ =

$5\frac{1}{4}$ ÷ $2\frac{1}{3}$ =

$3\frac{3}{5}$ X $2\frac{5}{6}$ =

$4\frac{1}{6}$ X $2\frac{2}{5}$ =

10

$\frac{2}{11}$

$\frac{2}{5}$

When people think of Alaska, many think of snow. But Alaska also has: active volcanoes, desert tundra, rain forest, 1/2 of the world's glaciers, North America's tallest mountain, swamps, 25-foot tall sand dunes, white water rivers, ice fields, permafrost, 3 million lakes and the Northern Lights!

Name _____

MULTIPLYING FRACTIONS & WHOLE NUMBERS

1. $\frac{4}{5}$ x 20 = $\frac{7}{12}$ x 12 = $\frac{2}{3}$ x 15 =

2. 7 x $\frac{1}{2}$ = $\frac{9}{10}$ x 15 = $\frac{3}{4}$ x 16 =

Review: Change these to improper fractions.

3. $5\frac{3}{7}$ = $9\frac{2}{3}$ = $6\frac{1}{8}$ =

Cancel. Then multiply.

4. $\frac{2}{3}$ X $\frac{3}{4}$ = $\frac{9}{10}$ X $\frac{5}{6}$ = $\frac{8}{20}$ X $\frac{4}{6}$ =

Reduce.

5. $\frac{25}{50}$ = $\frac{18}{34}$ = $\frac{180}{360}$ =

Divide.

6. $1\frac{5}{8} \div 1\frac{1}{4}$ = $\frac{3}{4} \div \frac{3}{8}$ = $\frac{4}{5} \div \frac{8}{9}$ =

7. $3\frac{1}{5} \div 2\frac{1}{7}$ = $1\frac{1}{10} \div 2\frac{1}{7}$ = $\frac{3}{4} \div 4\frac{1}{8}$ =

8. $2\frac{1}{2} \div 5$ = $7\frac{1}{3} \div 11$ = $8\frac{2}{3} \div 6\frac{1}{2}$ =

DIVISION OF FRACTIONS

1. $2\frac{1}{6} \div \frac{1}{3} =$ $3\frac{1}{2} \div \frac{1}{2} =$

2. $1\frac{1}{2} \div \frac{1}{4} =$ $2\frac{1}{3} \div 1\frac{1}{6} =$

3. $5\frac{2}{3} \div \frac{1}{3} =$ $6\frac{3}{4} \div 2\frac{1}{4} =$

Review.

4. $2\frac{1}{4} \times \frac{1}{3} =$ $4\frac{1}{2} \times \frac{2}{9} =$

5. $5\frac{2}{5} \times \frac{5}{9} =$ $\frac{7}{8} \times 4 =$

Change these to improper fractions.

6. $10\frac{1}{2} =$ $7\frac{1}{8} =$ $6\frac{1}{3} =$

7. $5\frac{4}{9} =$ $11\frac{3}{4} =$ $13\frac{2}{5} =$

Reduce.

8. $\frac{250}{300} =$ $\frac{48}{60} =$ $\frac{28}{35} =$

9. $\frac{44}{99} =$ $\frac{56}{16} =$ $\frac{95}{25} =$

10. $\frac{75}{225} =$ $\frac{64}{72} =$ $\frac{15}{225} =$

11. $\frac{10}{42} =$ $\frac{27}{117} =$ $\frac{54}{108} =$

OBJECTIVE: Review place value labels and reading and writing decimal fractions.

REVIEW: If you have already discussed the Base 10 System Wall Charts (pages 8-10) go over that material again for this lesson. If you have not used those pages, they fit with this lesson very well.

DEMONSTRATION

Place Value: The value of a numeral or digit depends upon the place it is located in the number.

Example: Tell students you have seven pieces of money, some coins and some paper money. (See the paper money on pages 11-16.) There is a 1 in the name of each. Which one would they like to have. Then write these amounts on the board: $10,000.00; $1000.00; $100.00; $10.00; $1.00; $.10; $.01.

Ask someone to read the amounts. Which one would they like to have? Why? Because the value is the greatest. The position or place of the 1 is very important. You can actually put the play money on the table, or just have seven empty, sealed envelopes with the amounts written on the front.

Go over the three wall charts (pages 8-10). Also, go over the wall chart on page 60.

HANDOUT: If you want students to have the wall charts in their math notebooks, use them as handouts at this time.

CLASSROOM DRILL: Read the numbers under the heading "Examples." Have students write them on scratch paper or the board. Point out that when they hear three-fourths, they write $\frac{3}{4}$. When they hear three thousandths, they write $\frac{3}{1000}$ or .003.

EXAMPLES: three tenths (.3), three hundreths (.03), three thousandths (.003), twenty-three hundreths (.23), twenty-three thousandths (.023), twenty-three ten thousandths (.0023), twenty-five thousand (25,000), twenty-five thousandths (.025), etc.

WORKSHEETS: When a number is written in words or powers of 10, that is called expanded form.

Example: three hundred or 3 x 10 to the second power or 3×10^2.

When a number is written in numerals or digits that is called standard form.

Example: 300

Powers of 10 have been mentioned on the wall charts. Go over that again if necessary:

$100 = 10 \times 10 = 10$ to the second power written 10^2.

$1000 = 10 \times 10 \times 10 = 10$ to the third power written 10^3.

You could generalize by saying the power of 10 tells how many zeros to put after the 1. For 6×10^3, you would write a 6 followed by 3 zeros.

OPTIONAL: DECIMAL DICE: If you were living in Alaska, there would be days when the temperature would be too low for you to go outside. (The record low is -83°F–that's temperature, not windchill.) Decimal Dice is a game you could play indoors with a friend or as a classroom tournament. See pages 65-67 for instructions, score sheets and a tournament brack-

1. **Look for the word *and*. The word *and* always stands for the decimal point.**

   a. If it is not in the written number, the number is either all whole numbers or all decimal fraction. (Example: thirteen thousand = 13,000; fifteen thousandths = .015)

   b. If the word *and* is in the written number, the number has both whole numbers and decimal fractions in it. (Example: twenty-four *and* two tenths = 24.2)

2. **Look for the *ths* at the end of the label word.**

   a. *ths* means that part of the number is a decimal fraction. (Example: eighteen thousandths is written .018 or $\frac{18}{1000}$.)

   b. No *ths* means that part of the number is a whole number. (Example: eighteen thousand is written 18,000.)

3. **To write a decimal fraction:**

   a. Write the decimal point and make a blank space for each place value up to the label. (Example: thirty-nine thousandths)

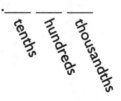

   b. Write the number with its last numeral in the last space to the right.

   $$.\underline{}\ \underline{3}\ \underline{9}$$

   c. Fill in with zeros all the way to the decimal point.

   $$.\underline{0}\ \underline{3}\ \underline{9}$$

Name ______________________________

RAINBOW MATH

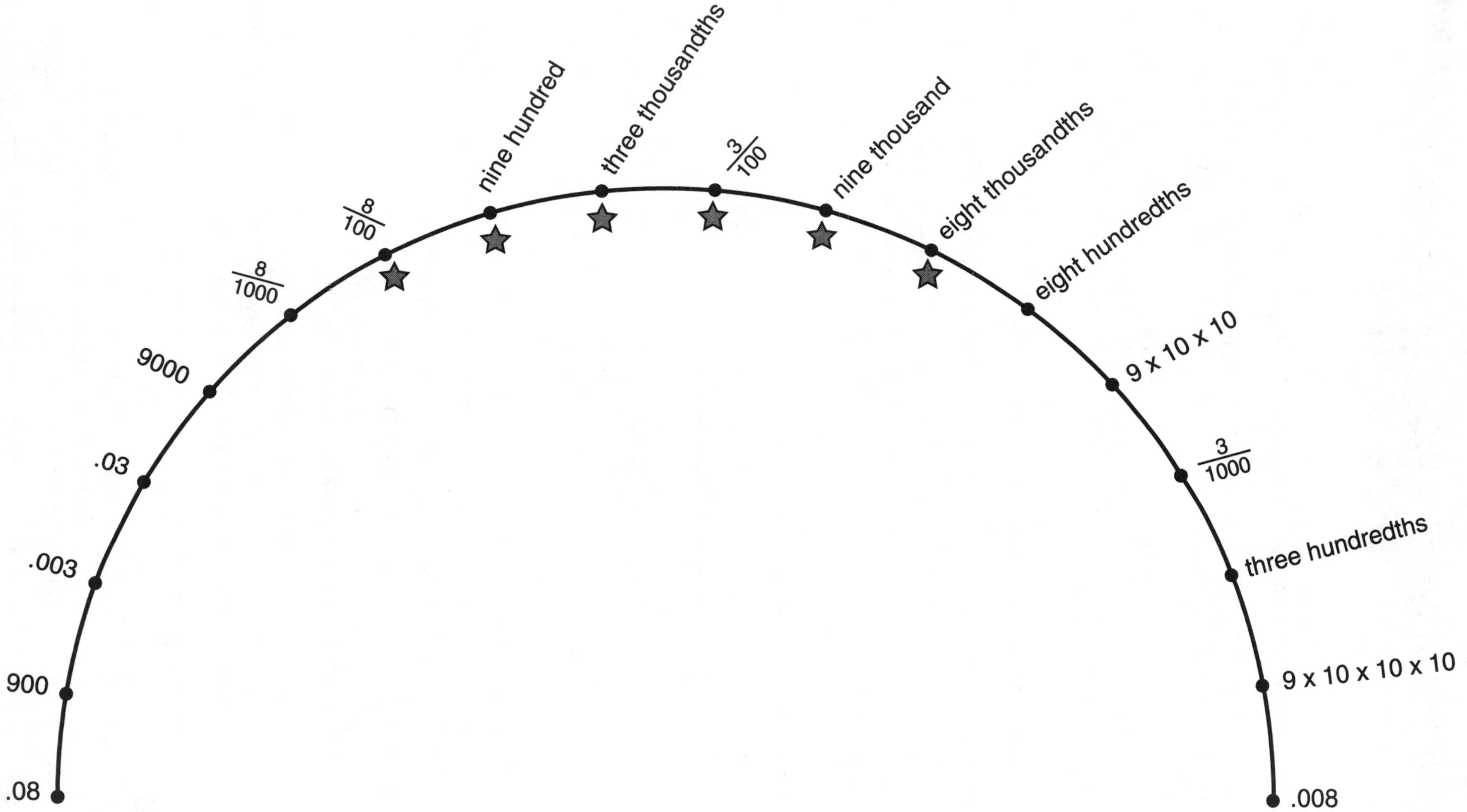
.08
900
.003
.03
9000
8/1000
8/100
nine hundred
three thousandths
3/100
nine thousand
eight thousandths
eight hundredths
9 x 10 x 10
3/1000
three hundredths
9 x 10 x 10 x 10
.008

Alaska is known for beautiful skies–aurora borealis by night and rainbows by day. Try this "rainbow-like" math art.

Each number with a star next to it has two equal numbers on the arc.

Draw two lines from each starred number–one to each number of equal value.

PLACE VALUE

Write each of these in standard form. Then shade or color the areas below which contain each of the answers. Remember that the word *and* is only used to represent the decimal point itself.

1. three hundred twenty-five _____.

2. three hundred twenty and five tenths _____.

3. three hundred and twenty-five hundredths _____.

4. three hundred twenty-five thousandths _____.

5. three and twenty-five thousandths _____.

6. three hundred twenty-five thousand _____.

7. thirty-two and five tenths _____.

8. thirty-two and five thousandths _____.

9. three and twenty-five hundredths _____.

10. three hundred twenty and five hundredths _____.

11. three hundred twenty and fifty-five hundredths _____.

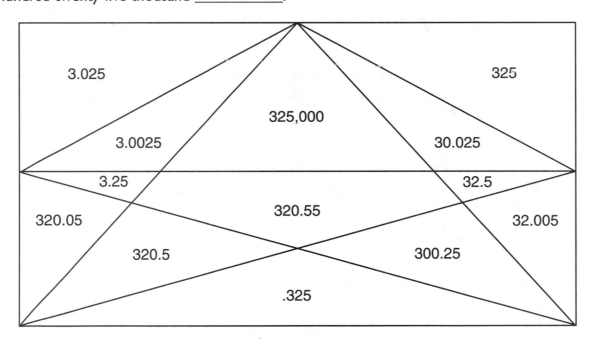

Write the numbers below on the back of this page and add.

11. Add these two numbers to find out how many rivers are in Alaska: one thousand one hundred twenty-three and five hundredths + one thousand eight hundred seventy-six and ninety-five hundredths = _____ rivers.

12. Add these two numbers to find the number of lakes in Alaska: one million two hundred fifteen thousand six hundred seventy-one + one million seven hundred eighty-four thousand three hundred twenty-nine = _____ lakes.

CHALLENGE:

Add these numbers to find the number of miles in Alaska's coastline: twenty-one thousand nine hundred seventy-eight and six tenths + ten thousand six hundred eighty-nine and thirty-two hundredths + three hundred thirty-two and eight hundreths = _____ miles in Alaska's coastline.

Name _____

BASE 10 SYSTEM

Write each number in standard form in the blank below each sentence. Then write each number horizontally in the grid. Do not add any decimal points.

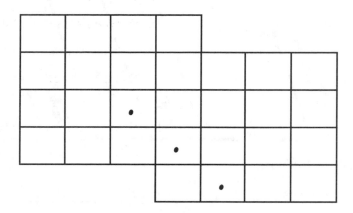

1. The United States bought Alaska from Czar Alexander of Russia for seven million two hundred thousand dollars. (Write this without the decimal point and two zeros.)

    _____

2. Port Walter on the Alaska Panhandle received two hundred twenty and nine thousandths of an inch of rain during one year.

    _____

3. The Alaska highway runs one thousand three hundred ninety-seven miles from Delta Junction, Alaska, to Dawson Creek, British Columbia.

    _____

4. According to the AAA Tour Book, Alaska has about one and four hundreths persons per square mile.

    _____

5. In Alaska's Glacier Bay National Monument, the famous Muir Glacier rises about eighty and eight ten-thousandths meters above the water.

    _____

CHALLENGE:
If Alaska has 586, 400 square miles and each square mile contains 640 acres, how many acres are contained in Alaska? _____

BASE 10 SYSTEM

Fill in the missing labels.

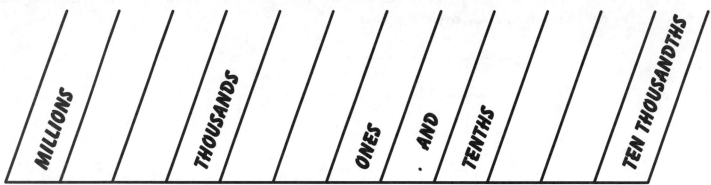

Write each number in standard form.

1. 10 thousands + two hundreds + 5 tens and 6 tenths ___10,250.6___

2. 2 hundreds + 3 ones and 2 tenths + 4 hundredths _____

3. 3 ten thousands + 5 thousands + one hundred and 8 hundreths _____

4. 6 hundred thousands + 5 tens and 9 thousandths _____

5. 5 millions + 2 tens and 4 ten thousandths _____

Write in expanded form.

6. 123.4 ___1 hundred + 2 tens + 3 ones and 4 tenths___

7. 50,040.003 _____

8. 6,004,100.02 _____

9. 32,600.008 _____

10. Mt. Mckinley, highest mountain in North American, stands 20,320 feet high. _____

11. Ten years ago, the U.S. census counted 550,043 people living in Alaska. _____

CHALLENGE:
Write this number using a power of 10. Alaska has 66,000,000 acres of undisturbed land. _____

DECIMAL DICE

Try this during the winter months when students are indoors for recess or during the last 10 minutes of class—if students have cooperated during classtime.

Two-player game.

Use two standard dice—cover the 1, 2 and 3 of one die with small pressure-sensitive stickers. Write 7, 8 and 9 on the stickers.

1. Use the Tournament Bracket on page 67.

2. Students draw numbers to see where they are placed on the bracket.

3. Students 1 and 2 play first unless they got in trouble during class.

4. One game consists of four sets (see score sheet on page 66).

5. One player chooses high or low for the first set and circles that word. Other player chooses high or low for the second set and so on.

6. Players write names in for each set.

7. First player rolls dice—puts the two numbers in two of the blank spaces. If *low* was circled, larger number should go to the right. If *high* was circled, larger numbers should go to the left in the larger place value slots.

8. Second player rolls and writes in the two numbers. Both players roll two more times. On the last roll, player may choose whichever number works best and ignore the other one.

9. Subtract smaller number from larger one in the space provided. Round off the answer to the nearest whole number.

10. If *high* was circled, the rounded off answer goes to the player with the higher score. If *low* was circled, the rounded off answer goes to the player with the lower score. Scores can vary wildly from 0 to 80 points.

11. Total each player's score after four sets. Write the winner's name on the next part of the bracket. Continue the process with the next set of students. Several games can be going on simultaneously.

12. If you have fewer than 32 students leave some parts of the bracket blank and give someone a pass to start if necessary.

DECIMAL DICE

SET 1 – HIGH OR LOW	Subtract	Points:
Name _____ # ___ ___ . ___ ___		Name:
Name _____ # ___ ___ . ___ ___ ___	Round to nearest whole number	

SET 2 – HIGH OR LOW	Subtract	Points:
Name _____ # ___ ___ . ___ ___		Name:
Name _____ # ___ ___ . ___ ___ ___	Round to nearest whole number	

SET 3 – HIGH OR LOW	Subtract	Points:
Name _____ # ___ ___ . ___ ___		Name:
Name _____ # ___ ___ . ___ ___ ___	Round to nearest whole number	

SET 4 – HIGH OR LOW	Subtract	Points:
Name _____ # ___ ___ . ___ ___		Name:
		Total points:
Name _____ # ___ ___ . ___ ___ ___	Round to nearest whole number	Name:

SET 1 – HIGH OR LOW	Subtract	Points:
Name _____ # ___ ___ . ___ ___		Name:
Name _____ # ___ ___ . ___ ___ ___	Round to nearest whole number	

SET 2 – HIGH OR LOW	Subtract	Points:
Name _____ # ___ ___ . ___ ___		Name:
Name _____ # ___ ___ . ___ ___ ___	Round to nearest whole number	

SET 3 – HIGH OR LOW	Subtract	Points:
Name _____ # ___ ___ . ___ ___		Name:
Name _____ # ___ ___ . ___ ___ ___	Round to nearest whole number	

SET 4 – HIGH OR LOW	Subtract	Points:
Name _____ # ___ ___ . ___ ___		Name:
		Total points:
Name _____ # ___ ___ . ___ ___ ___	Round to nearest whole number	Name:

OBJECTIVE: Review of decimal computation in preparation for more difficult problems.

DEMONSTRATION: Use Decimal Review (page 69) as an in-class worksheet. Talk about each group of problems and do the first in each group as a class. Have students do the others immediately and check as you go.

If you need help explaining some of the problems, use Lesson Plans 4 through 7 in *Math Phonics™–Decimals*.

HANDOUT: Use the wall charts (pages 33 and 55) from *Math Phonics™–Decimals* for a quick review. Have students try other examples like the ones on the wall charts.

CLASSROOM DRILL: Use the assessments (pages 88 and 89) from *Math Phonics™–Decimals* for extra practice.

WORKSHEET: After students have done page 69 together in class, collect the papers and give them another copy on page 69 to do as an at-home assignment. Then give the pre-assessment (page 70).

OPTIONAL: Have students make up another decimal review similar to page 69. Students will trade reviews and work the problems.

Name _____

DECIMAL REVIEW

Use this number: 164.59

1. Number in the tenths place _____

2. Number in the ones place _____

3. Number in the tens place _____

4. Number in the hundreds place _____

Write the decimal fraction for each.

5. $23\frac{4}{10} =$

6. $\frac{3}{100} =$

7. $\frac{50}{100} =$

8. $123\frac{5}{100} =$

9. How many quarters in a dollar? _____

10. How many nickels in a dollar? _____

Add or subtract.

11. $\begin{array}{r} 7.5 \\ + 9.8 \\ \hline \end{array}$

12. $\begin{array}{r} 25.3 \\ - 8.9 \\ \hline \end{array}$

13. $\begin{array}{r} 7.03 \\ - 4.29 \\ \hline \end{array}$

14. $\begin{array}{r} 29.8 \\ + 7.63 \\ \hline \end{array}$

Multiply.

15. $\begin{array}{r} 3.4 \\ \times\ .3 \\ \hline \end{array}$

16. $\begin{array}{r} 9.7 \\ \times\ .4 \\ \hline \end{array}$

17. $\begin{array}{r} .06 \\ \times\ 9 \\ \hline \end{array}$

18. $\begin{array}{r} 3.41 \\ \times\ 8 \\ \hline \end{array}$

19. $\begin{array}{r} 26.3 \\ \times\ .8 \\ \hline \end{array}$

Divide.

20. $4\overline{)3.6}$

21. $5\overline{).05}$

22. $.8\overline{)3.2}$

23. $1.3\overline{)2.86}$

Write each as a ratio.

24. 7 out of 10 students say cola is their favorite drink _____

25. 72 out of 100 students had the flu this month _____

Change to hundredths and a percent.

26. $\frac{3}{4} = \frac{}{100} = $ _____%

27. $\frac{4}{5} = \frac{}{100} = $ _____%

Divide to the hundredths place. Leave any remainder as a fraction.

28. $\frac{1}{2} = 2\overline{)1.00}$

29. $\frac{3}{15} =$

30. $\frac{7}{8} =$

DECIMAL PRE-ASSESSMENT

Use this number: 752.38

1. Number in the tenths place _____

2. Number in the tens place _____

3. Number in the ones place _____

4. Number in the hundreds place _____

Write the decimal fraction for each.

5. $2\frac{8}{10} =$

6. $\frac{4}{100} =$

7. $\frac{40}{100} =$

8. $21\frac{2}{100} =$

9. How many dimes in a dollar? _____

10. How many pennies in a dollar? _____

Add or subtract.

11. $\begin{array}{r} 8.4 \\ + 9.7 \\ \hline \end{array}$

12. $\begin{array}{r} 4.2 \\ - .9 \\ \hline \end{array}$

13. $\begin{array}{r} 6.04 \\ + 5.19 \\ \hline \end{array}$

14. $\begin{array}{r} 31.6 \\ + 4.23 \\ \hline \end{array}$

Multiply.

15. $\begin{array}{r} 2.3 \\ \times\ 4 \\ \hline \end{array}$

16. $\begin{array}{r} 4.7 \\ \times\ .2 \\ \hline \end{array}$

17. $\begin{array}{r} .04 \\ \times\ 9 \\ \hline \end{array}$

18. $\begin{array}{r} 2.25 \\ \times\ 3 \\ \hline \end{array}$

19. $\begin{array}{r} 24.8 \\ \times\ .4 \\ \hline \end{array}$

Divide.

20. $5\overline{)2.5}$

21. $4\overline{).04}$

22. $.6\overline{)2.4}$

23. $1.2\overline{)2.64}$

Write each as a ratio.

24. 4 out of 5 kids walk to school _____

25. 65 out of 100 students were at the game _____

Change to hundredths and percent.

26. $\frac{3}{5} = \frac{}{100} = $ _____%

27. $\frac{3}{4} = \frac{}{100} = $ _____%

Divide to the hundredths place. Leave any remainder as a fraction.

28. $\frac{1}{4} = 4\overline{)1.00}$

29. $\frac{7}{10} =$

30. $\frac{5}{8} =$

LESSON PLAN 7: ADDING & SUBTRACTING DECIMAL FRACTIONS

OBJECTIVE: Build on what students have already learned and try some harder problems in addition and subtraction.

REVIEW: Go over adding and subtracting fractions. Remind students that common denominators are necessary in order to add or subtract.

DEMONSTRATION: Students should already have learned that decimals must be in a straight line for addition and subtraction. For help in explaining why this is done, use Lesson Plan 4 in *Math Phonics™– Decimals*.

Talking about money can also help with this concept. When adding money, the decimals are in a straight line so that you are adding dimes to dimes and pennies to pennies.

HANDOUT: If you have not already passed out copies of the wall chart on page 33 of *Math Phonics™–Decimals*, do so now. Go over this carefully.

CLASSROOM DRILL: Read problems from worksheets (pages 72-73). This will give students practice in writing decimal fractions correctly. Have students do these at their desks or at the board.

WORKSHEET: Mention to students that some numbers do not have a decimal point–25 would be one example. Ask them where they could put a decimal point without changing the value of the number. It always goes to the right of the number. When the decimal is in place, zeros may be added without changing the value.

OPTIONAL: Use the worksheets on pages 74 and 75 if needed.

Name _____

ADDING DECIMALS

Put the decimal point in the correct place.

1.
$$4.8$$
$$+\ 7.9$$
$$\overline{127}$$

$5 + .03 = 503$

$19 + 1.6 = 206$

$25.5 + 10.5 = 360$

$100.8 + 100.1 = 2009$

Add.

2.
$$7.4$$
$$9.8$$
$$+\ .7$$

$$8.3$$
$$6.9$$
$$+\ .6$$

$$28.92$$
$$+\ \ 3.82$$

$$89.81$$
$$37.29$$
$$+\ \ 4.47$$

$$31.68$$
$$94.79$$
$$+\ \ 8.57$$

Add or subtract. Reduce answers to lowest terms.

3. $24\frac{1}{7}$
$\quad -\ 15\frac{2}{3}$

$\overline{\qquad}$
$27\frac{7}{10}$

$+39\frac{3}{4}$

$43\frac{3}{5}$
$-\ 18\frac{5}{6}$

Multiply or divide. Reduce answers to lowest terms.

4. $\frac{1}{2} \times \frac{6}{5} =$

$\frac{1}{2} \div \frac{1}{6} =$

$1\frac{6}{10} \div \frac{4}{5} =$

5. You will be staying in Banff Springs to do a little skiing. The snow base was 29.8 inches two days ago. It increased 5.03 inches yesterday and 6 inches so far today. What is the total snow base? _____

6. The closest ski lodge rents skis and poles for $12.50 per day, boots for $15 per day and lift tickets are $25.75 per day. How much will it cost for 2 days of skiing? _____

CHALLENGE:
Your tour guide loves to make up puzzles. He says the cost of one day of skiing for the entire group is a four-digit number with no zeros. The largest place value is thousands. It is the smallest number you can make using four consecutive digits. What is the cost? _____

SUBTRACTING DECIMALS

Subtract. Keep decimal points in a straight line.

1.
$$\begin{array}{r} 3.5 \\ -\ .7 \\ \hline \end{array}$$
$$\begin{array}{r} 37.1 \\ -\ 22.2 \\ \hline \end{array}$$
$$\begin{array}{r} 127.3 \\ -\ 39.8 \\ \hline \end{array}$$
$$\begin{array}{r} 101.78 \\ -\ 90.49 \\ \hline \end{array}$$
$5.6 - .3 =$

$12.5 - 6 =$

Keep decimal points in a straight line.

2. $.07 + .21 + 5 =$

   $31 + 5.8 + 2.1 =$

$$\begin{array}{r} 23.78 \\ 91.09 \\ +\ 4.86 \\ \hline \end{array}$$

$$\begin{array}{r} 19.072 \\ 98.334 \\ +\ 16.279 \\ \hline \end{array}$$

Multiply or divide. Reduce answers.

3. $3\frac{3}{4} \times \frac{2}{3} =$ $\frac{4}{5} \times \frac{15}{16} =$ $4\frac{1}{8} \div \frac{3}{4} =$

4. $\frac{1}{4} \div \frac{3}{4} =$ $1\frac{5}{8} \div 1\frac{1}{4} =$ $1\frac{7}{10} \div \frac{4}{5} =$

5. In the winter, some float plane owners remove the floats and attach skis so they can land in the snow. If 2 floats weigh 47.14 pounds each and skis weigh 19.7 pounds each, how much lighter is the plane with skis? _____

6. You are watching altitude markers while skiing. The last one was 10,231.8 feet and this one is 9,863.07 feet. How many feet have you descended? _____

CHALLENGE:

Your tour guide has offered $5 to the first person who can solve his puzzle: How much was lunch for four people at the ski lodge: It is a four-digit number with the 10s place as the largest place value. No zeros. It is the largest using four consecutive digits with the digit 3 in the 1s place. _____

MORE DECIMAL ADDITION PRACTICE

1.
$13.26	$18.50	$46.87	$34.00	$358.26
15.90	9.26	52.39	17.98	37.18
+ 12.00	+ .25	+ 11.12	+ 19.42	+ .35

2.
1.3	2.5	34.97	35.148	18.083
2.4	4.7	1.06	7.915	9.136
+ 1.9	+ 8.9	+ 5.93	+ 13.067	+ 28.391

3.
.88	1.82	8.00	1213.2	1.427
.31	3.71	16.92	348.6	3.891
+ .56	+ 9.13	+ 4.88	+ 24.9	+ 5.624

4. $3.8 + 4.12 + 6.359 =$

5. $48 + .73 + 21.6 =$

6. $24.5 + 18.01 + 2.739 =$

7. $123 + 4.86 + 17.001 =$

8. $27.9 + 16 + 5.04 =$

9. $45.6 + 25 + 13.026 =$

Name _____

MORE DECIMAL SUBTRACTION PRACTICE

1.
2.4	25.0	$5.37	4.001	423.8
- .9	- 17.5	- 3.98	- .002	- 319.9

2.
203.04	$2341.18	15.638	.7402	31.604
- 12.09	- 1968.27	- 4.801	- .3814	- 20.403

3.
3.162	243.9	30.123	15.126	241.06
- .084	- 27.6	- 18.071	- 9.041	- 28.71

4. 16.03 - .142 =

5. .076 - .042 =

6. 26.183 - 5.6 =

7. 63.7 - 50.12 =

8. $100.75 - $16.48 =

9. 763.8 - 5.062 =

OBJECTIVE: Practicing skills learned earlier and learning new skills and "tricks" in multiplying and dividing decimals.

REVIEW: Go over the wall charts from *Math Phonics™–Decimals* (pages 33 and 55) if necessary.

DEMONSTRATION: In *Math Phonics™–Multiplication* (pages 53 and 58) students are taught quick ways to multiply by 10 and 100.

When we add a 0 to a number to multiply by 10, we are actually moving the decimal point one place to the right.

$$5 \times 10 = 50 \qquad 5 \times 10 = 5.0$$

When we add two 0s to multiply by 100, we are moving the decimal point two places to the right.

$$5 \times 100 = 500 \qquad 5 \times 100 = 5.00$$

In *Math Phonics™–Division* (page 67) students are taught that to divide by 100, drop two 0s. By doing this, we are actually moving the decimal point two places to the left.

$$300 \div 100 = 3.00$$

If you can't remember which way to move the decimal, just remember that to divide by 100, the answer will be smaller than the original number (500).

$$500 \div 100 = 5.00 = 5$$

To multiply by 100, the answer will be larger than the original number.

$$500 \times 100 = 500.00 = 50,000$$

To multiply or divide by 1000, move the decimal point three places.

$$3 \times 1000 = 3.000$$

$$3 \div 1000 = .003$$

This makes sense because a fraction means "divide" so

$$3 \div 1000 = \tfrac{3}{1000} \quad .0\ 0\ 3 \text{ thousandths}$$

POWERS OF 10: Refer to the wall chart on page 8 in this book. Notice that the hundreds place is labeled with 100, 10 x 10 and 10^2. This is read 10 squared or 10 to the second power. You can also multiply by powers of 10. If you multiply a number by 10^2, you move the decimal point two places.

Sometimes a problem has three factors and two of them have a product of 100. Learn to do these as mental math. Worksheet X (page 80).

Example 1: 3 x 2 x 50 = ? (2 x 50 = 100)
    3 x 100 = 300

Example 2: 2 x 4 x 25 = ? (4 x 25 = 100)
    2 x 100 = 200

REPEATING DECIMALS: Page 83. When some numbers are divided, the answer never comes out "even." These are referred to as repeating decimals. (If a decimal never repeats, it is called an irrational number. We will not study those in this book.)

Example 1: $\frac{1}{11}$ =

$$11\overline{)1.000000}^{\,.090909\,...}$$

    99

    100
     99

    100

Place a bar over the numbers that repeat.

$$\frac{1}{11} = .\overline{09}$$

HANDOUT: Pages 79 and 80 can be used for in-class practice. Be sure they know that they can use the same numbers for all in the first row—they just need to see where to put the decimal point.

Explain this example:

$$34 \times 2 = 68$$
$$3.4 \times 2 = 6.8$$
$$3.4 \times .2 = .68$$
$$.34 \times .02 = .0068$$

The answer has four decimal places. The zero for the extra decimal place goes to the left of the number here's why:

$$.34 = \frac{34}{100} \quad .02 = \frac{2}{100}$$
$$\frac{34}{100} \times \frac{2}{100} = \frac{68}{10,000} = .0068$$

Have students do one row and then check. Explain as needed as you go.

CLASSROOM DRILL: For page 82, work on the first few problems as a class so students understand how to add a decimal point and zeros to divide.

$$2\overline{)35.0}^{\,17.5} \qquad \begin{array}{r} \text{check} \\ 17.5 \\ \times\ 2 \\ \hline 35.0 \end{array}$$

    2

    15
    14

    10

$$6\overline{)51.0}^{\,8.5} \qquad \begin{array}{r} \text{check} \\ 8.5 \\ \times\ 6 \\ \hline 51.0 \end{array}$$

    48

    30

WORKSHEETS: Hand out another copy of pages 79 and 80 to be used as assignments. For page 81, go over a few examples like the mental math. Teach students to multiply the non-zero numbers and then add as many zeros as the total in the problem.

Example:

Old Way

$$\begin{array}{r} 20 \\ \times\ 30 \\ \hline 00 \\ 60 \\ \hline 600 \end{array}$$

New Way

20 x 30 = 600

Think: 2 x 3 = 6, two 0s in the problem, two 0s in the answer.

OPTIONAL: Run off a set of multiplication flash cards (pages 29-37 in *Math Phonics™—Multiplication*). For some, add decimals and for others, add zeros to make more challenging problems for kids to use for drill.

Example:

Flash card says:	Flash card says:
1 x 6 = 6	6 x 7 = 42
Change it	Change it
.1 x 6 = .6	60 x 70 = 4200

NOTE: In word problems, *of* means "times." When a problem says .67 of the days, for example, you would take .67 times the number of days.

DECIMAL MULTIPLICATION

Do these in your head if possible. Use scratch paper if necessary.

1. 23 x 2 =   2.3 x 2 =   .23 x 2 =   .23 x .2 =

2. 71 x 5 =   7.1 x 5 =   7.1 x .5 =   .71 x .5 =

3.   14   14   .14   14
     x 11   x 1.1   x 1.1   x .11

4.   55   5.5   .55   .55
     x 9   x 9   x .9   x .09

5.   9.9   .99   8.8   .88
     x 4   x .4   x 3.3   x 3.3

6.   123   12.3   34.6   3.46
     x 7.8   x .78   x 3.4   x .34

Put decimals in the correct places.

7. 35.21 x 18 = 63378   3521 x .18 = 63378   3.521 x 1.8 = 63378

8. 72.81 x 6 = 43686   7.281 x .6 = 43686   .7281 x .6 = 43686

9. .2 x 12 =   4 x .8 =   .6 x .6 =

10. 25 x .2 =   .8 x .02 =   25 x .3 =

POWERS OF 10—MULTIPLICATION

Move the decimal one place for each zero.

1. $7 \times 10 =$ $7 \times 100 =$ $8 \times 10 =$ $8 \times 1000 =$

2. $7.1 \times 10 =$ $7.1 \times 100 =$ $8.3 \times 10 =$ $8.3 \times 1000 =$

3. $9 \times 10 =$ $9 \times 100 =$ $9 \times 1000 =$ $9 \times 10,000 =$

4. $9 \times 2 \times 5 =$ $9 \times 10 \times 10 =$ $9 \times 10 \times 10 \times 10 =$

Learn these factors of 100.

5.   25   20   50   10
       $\times\ 4$ $\times\ 5$ $\times\ 2$ $\times\ 10$

Look for factors of 100.

6. $2 \times 4 \times 25 =$ $6 \times 5 \times 20 =$ $9 \times 2 \times 50 =$

7. $2 \times 100 =$ $6 \times 100 =$ $9 \times 100 =$

8. $7 \times 10 \times 10 =$ $8 \times 2 \times 50 =$ $5 \times 4 \times 25 =$

9. $2 \times 3 \times 50 =$ $4 \times 6 \times 25 =$ $2 \times 7 \times 50 =$

If the power of 10 is 2, add two 0s or move the decimal two places.

10. $10 \times 10 = 10^2 =$ $10 \times 10 \times 10 = 10^3 =$

11. $5 \times 10^2 =$ $3 \times 10^2 =$ $7 \times 10^3 =$

12. $4 \times 10^3 =$ $8 \times 10^4 =$ $9 \times 10^5 =$

13. $5.5 \times 10^2 =$ $4 \times 8 \times 100 =$ $7.2 \times 10^3 =$

14. $4.9 \times 10^3 =$ $.98 \times 10^2 =$ $.23 \times 10^3 =$

POWERS OF 10-DIVISION

Move the decimal point one place for each zero or power of 10.

1. $50 \div 10 =$ $500 \div 10 =$ $500 \div 100 =$

2. $55 \div 10 =$ $550 \div 10 =$ $550 \div 100 =$

3. $200 \div 10^2 =$ $300 \div 10 =$ $300 \div 10^2 =$

4. $9.3 \div 10 =$ $7.4 \div 100 =$ $8.4 \div 10^2 =$

Do these in your head.

5. $20 \times 40 =$ $70 \times 50 =$ $60 \times 800 =$

6. $90 \times 80 =$ $400 \times 800 =$

Review.

7.   9.24   87.3   14.82
     x 2.3   x 3.9   x 7.4

8. Alaska is know for its glaciers. It has half of all the glaciers in the world! Write 10^5 with all the zeros—that is known as standard notation. _____

9. Alaska's volcanoes have earned it the name "Land of 10,000 Smokes." Write 10,000 using power of 10. _____

CHALLENGE:

The temperature has dropped to -80°F. Arthur is very low. Who is Arthur? Work these problems and then decode the secret answer below.

B = .4   C = .5
D = .3   F = .9

.4 x B =	D x F =	.3 x C =	B x F =
T	*M*	*R*	*O*
.2 x D =	.2 x F =	B x C =	D x B =
H	*A*	*E*	*U*

___ ___ ___ ___ ___ ___
.18 .15 .16 .06 .12 .15

___ ___ ___ ___ ___ ___ ___
.27 .36 .27 .20 .16 .20 .15

DECIMAL DIVISION

Add decimal point and zeros if needed. Divide until the answer comes out even. Check.

1.

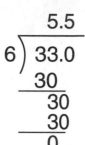

$$\begin{array}{r} 5.5 \\ 6\,\overline{)33.0} \\ \underline{30} \\ 30 \\ \underline{30} \\ 0 \end{array}$$

Check.
$$\begin{array}{r} 5.5 \\ \times\ 6 \\ \hline 33.0 \end{array}$$

$2\,\overline{)35}$

$6\,\overline{)51}$

2.

$5\,\overline{)42}$

$12\,\overline{)498}$

$28\,\overline{)602}$

Put decimal point directly above decimal point in the bracket. Check.

3.

$7\,\overline{)86.1}$

$14\,\overline{)16.8}$

$61\,\overline{)128.1}$

Move decimal in divisor to make it a whole number. Move decimal inside the bracket the same number of places. Divide. Check.

4.

$3.9\,\overline{)89.7}$

$.41\,\overline{)131.2}$

$5.6\,\overline{)190.4}$

DECIMAL DIVISION

Make a division problem out of each fraction. Write the division answer as a fraction and reduce.

$$\frac{1}{4} = 1 \div 4 = 4\overline{)1.00} \quad \begin{array}{r} .25 \\ \underline{8} \\ 20 \\ \underline{20} \\ 0 \end{array}$$

$$.25 = \frac{25 \div 5}{100 \div 5} = \frac{5 \div 5}{20 \div 5} = \frac{1}{4}$$

1. $\frac{1}{5} =$

2. $\frac{1}{2} =$

3. $\frac{3}{5} =$

Repeating decimals. Put a bar over the numeral or numerals that repeat.

4. $\frac{1}{3} =$ $\frac{1}{6} =$

5. $\frac{1}{9} =$ $\frac{3}{11} =$

6. Your friend, Benny, will be competing in the Iditarod* sled dog race. His 12 dogs eat about 3.8 pounds of food each day. How much dog food will he need for 3 days? _____

7. The sled weighs about 586 pounds. If .9 of that is for food, how much does the food weigh? _____

CHALLENGE:
The Iditarod Trail is about 1049 miles long. If a driver or musher, can cover .67 of the trail in the first 5 days, how many miles will be left in the race? _____

*This race memorializes the life-saving trip from Anchorage to Nome in 1925. Mushers made the trip carrying the diphtheria vaccine, saving many lives.

LESSON PLAN 9: FRACTIONS, DECIMALS, RATIOS & PERCENTS

OBJECTIVE: Show the relationships among fractions, ratios, decimals and percents. Introduce cross-multiplication and percents less than 1% and more than 100%.

REVIEW: Use Lesson Plans 8 and 9 in *Math Phonics™–Decimals* if students need to review the basics. Briefly, fractions can be expressed as decimals, ratios and percents.

Example:

$$\frac{1}{4} = \frac{25}{100} = .25 = 25\% = 4\overline{)1.00}$$

$$\begin{array}{r} .25 \\ 4\overline{)1.00} \\ \underline{8} \\ 20 \end{array}$$

DEMONSTRATION: Simple ratios can be set up like equivalent fractions and solved by cross multiplication. When two ratios are equal, their cross-products are equal.

Check.

$$\frac{3 \text{ x } 3}{4 \text{ x } 3} = \frac{x}{12}$$

$$x = 9$$

$$\frac{3}{4} \diagdown \frac{9}{12}$$

$$4 \times 9 = 36$$
$$3 \times 12 = 36$$

Don't confuse this with cancelling. With cancelling, you are dividing something above the line and something below the line by the same number. Example:

$$\frac{\overset{1}{\cancel{6}} \times \overset{1}{\cancel{2}}}{\underset{3}{\cancel{6}} \times \underset{1}{\cancel{6}}} = \frac{1}{3}$$

This all takes place on the same side of the equal sign.

With cross-multiplication, the multiplying crosses over the equal sign.

$$\frac{3}{4} \diagup\!\!\!\!\diagdown \frac{6}{8}$$

$$4 \times 6 = 24$$
$$3 \times 8 = 24$$

HANDOUT: Worksheet BB (page 86). Do one example so students understand. Make up a tally. (Be sure they know that *tally* means "small marks to keep track of a score or other items.") Use 4 as the tally for the r. The ratio is 4 out of 100 or $\frac{4}{100}$. The decimal is .04 and the percent is 4%. Some students could start on line 2 or 3 so there will be some variety in the answers.

CLASSROOM DRILL: Percents less than 1 and more than 100. Some people confuse $\frac{1}{2}$% and 50%. Use page 17 in *Math Phonics™–Decimals*. Run off two copies. Have someone shade in $\frac{1}{2}$ of one of the squares. That is 50%. On the other copy, have someone shade in 50 of the small squares. That is 50%.

For an explanation of how to use the table on page 88, refer to *Math Phonics™–Decimals*, page 81 and worksheet, page 83. Briefly, 10% of a number is found by moving the decimal one place to the left. Move the decimal point one more place to the left for 1%. For $\frac{1}{2}$%, take half of the 1%. For 50% of a number, divide the number by 2. For 150%, add the number plus half of the number.

Example:

	10%	1%	$\frac{1}{2}$%
600	60	6	3

Example:

	50%	150%
600	300	900

WORKSHEETS: For Worksheet CC (page 87), use sample word problems.

For #6, 2 out of 3 people in the school came down with the flu. If there are 300 people in the school, how many got the flu?

$$\frac{2}{3} \times \frac{100}{100} = \frac{x}{300}$$

x = 200 got the flu

For #7, if 70% of the people like hamburgers and there are 50 in the group, how many like hamburgers?

$$\frac{70 \div 2}{100 \div 2} = \frac{x}{50}$$

x = 35 like hamburgers

PERCENTS

Read the Pledge of Allegiance and write the letters—one in each square. Do not leave any blank spaces. Tally the number of times each letter appears and complete the table below.

I pledge allegiance to the flag of the United States of America and to the Republic for which it stands, one Nation under God, indivisible, with liberty and justice for all.

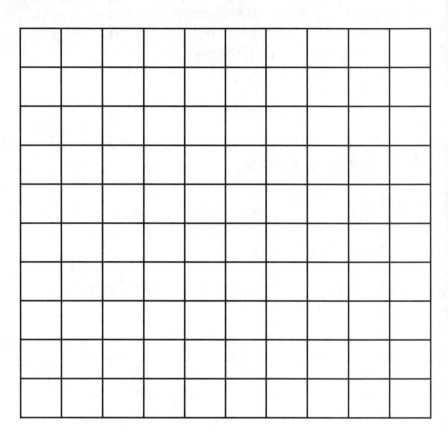

LETTER	R	S	T	L	N	E
TALLY						
RATIO						
DECIMAL						
PERCENT						

Name _____

RATIOS

Complete each ratio using the equivalent fraction method. Check by cross-multiplying.

1.
$$\frac{2 \times 5}{3 \times 5} = \frac{X}{15}$$

Check.

$$\frac{2}{3} \times \frac{10}{15}$$

$x = 10$

$2 \times 15 = 30$
$3 \times 10 = 3$

$$\frac{2}{5} = \frac{X}{10}$$

$$\frac{1}{2} = \frac{X}{14}$$

2.
$$\frac{3}{100} = \frac{X}{300}$$

$$\frac{5}{100} = \frac{X}{300}$$

$$\frac{6}{100} = \frac{X}{400}$$

Review.

3. $30 \times 60 =$ $80 \times 10^2 =$ $7 \times 300 =$

4. $2.5 \times 100 =$ $5 \times 8 \times 20 =$ $600 \times 70 =$

5.
$$7\overline{)36.4}$$ $$3.2\overline{)115.2}$$ $$1.8\overline{)73.8}$$

6. Three out of four people in your tour group suffered minor frostbite. If there are 24 in the group, how many got frostbite? _____

7. You are visiting with a group of families who live in Alaska's bush country (the last frontier). One man comments that 60% of "bush families" never use light bulbs. If there are 50 families present, how many of them do not use light bulbs? _____

CHALLENGE:
In another group of bush families, 80% never get a water bill—they live near a river. If 32 families don't get a water bill, what's the total number of families in that group? _____

PERCENTS

Complete this table.

NUMBER	10%	1%	1/2%	50%	150%
200					
400					
800					

1. $\dfrac{2}{20} = \dfrac{X}{100}$ $\dfrac{5}{25} = \dfrac{X}{100}$ $\dfrac{15}{50} = \dfrac{X}{100}$

2. $\dfrac{16}{20} = \dfrac{X}{100}$ $\dfrac{35}{50} = \dfrac{X}{100}$ $\dfrac{45}{50} = \dfrac{X}{100}$

Review. Put a bar over the repeating numerals.

3.

   $\dfrac{2}{3} = \quad 3\overline{)2}$ $\dfrac{5}{6} = \quad 6\overline{)5}$

4. Alaska has approximately 600,000 people. You are helping with a survey about changing the name of Mt. McKinley back to Denali, the Athabascan word meaning "the great one." You hope to reach $\frac{1}{2}$% of the people. How many people do you hope to reach? _____

5. It is believed that with a few improvements in services, Alaska's population could quickly grow to 150% of the present number. If that happened, how many people would then live in Alaska? _____

CHALLENGE:
Your friend says Alaska has thirty hundred rivers. How do you write that number? _____

You may want to run off copies of some of these pages of rules for students to put in their math notebooks.

Basic Math Facts
Page 20 in this book.

Fractions
Math Phonics™–Fractions–page 89

Decimals
Math Phonics™–Decimals–page 87

Writing Decimal Fractions
Page 60 in this book.

GAMES

Cinco–page 30 in this book.

Decimal Dice–pages 65-67 in this book

Math Phonics™–Fractions
    Fraction Bingo–page 39
    Fraction Slapjack–page 39
    Fraction Action–page 55
    Improper Fraction Slapjack–page 61

Math Phonics™–Decimals
    Decimal Bingo–page 19
    Decimal Flash Cards–pages 20-23

BIBLIOGRAPHY

A Child's Alaska by Claire Rudolf Murphy. Alaska Northwest Books, 1994.

Alaska by Joyce Johnston. Lerner Publications, 1994.

From Sea to Shining Sea–Alaska by Dennis Brindell Fradin. Children's Press–a division of Grolier Publishing, 1993.

Here Is . . . Alaska written and published by J & H Sales, no year given.

In Denali by Kim Heacox. Companion Press, 1992.

The Story of Seward's Folly by Susan Clinton. Children's Press, 1987.

Tour Book–AAA, AAA Publishing, 2001.

FRACTIONS

1.
$\frac{7}{8}$
$+ \frac{7}{8}$
          $1\frac{2}{3}$
$+ 1\frac{2}{3}$
          $13\frac{3}{4}$
$+ 8\frac{2}{3}$
          $6\frac{1}{5}$
$+ 9\frac{2}{3}$
          $7\frac{5}{6}$
$+ 8\frac{1}{7}$

2.
$\frac{5}{6}$
$- \frac{1}{6}$
          $\frac{7}{9}$
$- \frac{1}{2}$
          $\frac{3}{4}$
$- \frac{2}{3}$
          $10\frac{1}{8}$
$- 7\frac{1}{4}$
          $16\frac{1}{5}$
$- 9\frac{3}{4}$

3. $\frac{3}{4} \times \frac{8}{9} =$ $1\frac{1}{4} \times 1\frac{1}{4} =$ $3\frac{3}{4} \times \frac{1}{3} =$

4. $\frac{5}{6} \times \frac{18}{20} =$ $\frac{1}{3} \times 15\frac{3}{4} =$ $4\frac{7}{10} \times \frac{5}{9} =$

5. $\frac{2}{3} \div \frac{4}{9} =$ $\frac{4}{5} \div 1\frac{1}{5} =$ $6 \div \frac{1}{5} =$

6. $\frac{3}{4} \div 3\frac{1}{8} =$ $5\frac{1}{4} \div 2\frac{1}{3} =$ $1\frac{7}{8} \div 1\frac{1}{4} =$

DECIMALS

1. $25.01 + 1.6 + 18 =$ $\begin{array}{r} 38.4 \\ + \ 27.98 \\ \hline \end{array}$ $\begin{array}{r} 15.24 \\ 7.96 \\ + \ 8.21 \\ \hline \end{array}$ $\begin{array}{r} 35.76 \\ 91.03 \\ + \ 4.7 \\ \hline \end{array}$

2. $\begin{array}{r} \$49.06 \\ - \ 17.28 \\ \hline \end{array}$ $236 - 1.08 =$ $\begin{array}{r} 18.126 \\ - \ 9.873 \\ \hline \end{array}$ $\begin{array}{r} 238.71 \\ + \ 90.68 \\ \hline \end{array}$

3. $\begin{array}{r} 15 \\ \times \ 2.1 \\ \hline \end{array}$ $\begin{array}{r} 29 \\ \times \ .04 \\ \hline \end{array}$ $\begin{array}{r} 8.8 \\ \times \ 2.3 \\ \hline \end{array}$ $\begin{array}{r} 3.21 \\ \times \ .34 \\ \hline \end{array}$ $\begin{array}{r} 72.1 \\ \times \ 3.5 \\ \hline \end{array}$

4.

$6 \overline{)\ 57}$ $5 \overline{)\ 63}$ $7 \overline{)\ 51.1}$ $.24 \overline{)\ 4.8}$

Find X. Check by cross multiplication.

5. $\dfrac{20}{25} = \dfrac{X}{100}$ $\dfrac{2}{5} = \dfrac{X}{25}$ $\dfrac{3}{4} = \dfrac{X}{36}$

6. $10\% \text{ of } 450 =$ $1\% \text{ of } 300 =$

7. $20 \times 80 =$ $3 \times 4 \times 25 =$ $6 \times 10^3 =$

8. $500 \div 10 =$ $4.3 \div 100 =$ $300 \div 10^2 =$

Divide to find the decimal value. Put a bar over the repeating decimal.

9. $\dfrac{3}{4} =$ $\dfrac{4}{5} =$ $\dfrac{5}{6} =$

BASE 10 COUNTING CHART

1	2	3	4	5	6	7	8	9	10
11	12	13	14	15	16	17	18	19	20
21	22	23	24	25	26	27	28	29	30
31	32	33	34	35	36	37	38	39	40
41	42	43	44	45	46	47	48	49	50
51	52	53	54	55	56	57	58	59	60
61	62	63	64	65	66	67	68	69	70
71	72	73	74	75	76	77	78	79	80
81	82	83	84	85	86	87	88	89	90
91	92	93	94	95	96	97	98	99	100
101	102	103	104	105	106	107	108	109	110
111	112	113	114	115	116	117	118	119	120
121	122	123	124	125	126	127	128	129	130
131	132	133	134	135	136	137	138	139	140
141	142	143	144	145	146	147	148	149	150

Pre-Assessment, page 26
1. 12, 11, 16, 18, 13
2. 14, 15, 11, 12, 14
3. 15, 12, 13, 11, 16
4. 12, 17, 13, 14, 11
5. 9, 8, 9, 3, 8, 5
6. 4, 6, 8, 8, 4, 9
7. 4, 3, 7, 7, 7, 5
8. 9, 5, 2, 8, 6, 6
9. 5, 6, 6, 8, 9, 7
10. 9, 9, 8, 7, 7, 9

Pre-Assessment, page 27
1. 16, 30, 49, 9, 36, 64, 27
2. 18, 35, 20, 36, 12, 42, 45
3. 56, 48, 15, 25, 24, 63, 81
4. 32, 24, 40, 54, 72, 21, 28
5. 6, 8, 9, 7, 5, 7, 4, 4
6. 6, 6, 8, 8, 4, 5, 5, 4
7. 3, 6, 7, 6, 7, 9, 9, 5
8. 8, 4, 5, 4, 9, 4, 6, 3
9. 8, 8, 4, 3, 7, 9, 6, 3
10. 5, 3, 7, 8, 9, 5, 3, 9

Fraction Review, page 38
1. $\frac{1}{4}, \frac{1}{3}, \frac{2}{5}, \frac{2}{3}, \frac{2}{3}$
2. 12, 28, 12, 16, 40
3. $3\frac{1}{3}, 7\frac{1}{2}, 3\frac{1}{7}, 1\frac{5}{8}$
4. $\frac{2}{3}, \frac{3}{8}, 25\frac{5}{14}, 5\frac{7}{10}, 37\frac{20}{21}$
5. $\frac{21}{8}, \frac{21}{4}, \frac{19}{3},$
6. $\frac{1}{15}, \frac{3}{20}, \frac{3}{20}, \frac{1}{5}$
7. 3, 3, 4

Fraction Pre-Assessment, page 39
1. $\frac{3}{5}, \frac{1}{3}, \frac{2}{3}, \frac{7}{8}, \frac{2}{5}$
2. 5, 9, 3, 56, 40
3. $1\frac{3}{4}, 1\frac{4}{7}, 1\frac{11}{12}, 4\frac{3}{4}, 2\frac{4}{11}$
4. $\frac{7}{3}, \frac{11}{4}, \frac{16}{3}, \frac{35}{6}, \frac{37}{5}$
5. $\frac{2}{4} = \frac{1}{2}, \frac{3}{4}, \frac{3}{8}, \frac{4}{9}, \frac{14}{10} = 1\frac{2}{5}$
6. $\frac{1}{6}, \frac{1}{20}, \frac{8}{15}, \frac{5}{8}$
7. 4, 2, 5, $\frac{7}{5} = 1\frac{2}{5}$

Worksheet A, page 42
1959

Worksheet B, page 43
1. $\frac{3}{5}, \frac{3}{5}, \frac{1}{3}, \frac{3}{4}, \frac{5}{9}$
2. $6\frac{1}{6}, 11\frac{2}{7}$
3. $6\frac{1}{5}, 10\frac{5}{7}, 9\frac{2}{3}, 19\frac{2}{9}$
4. $4\frac{3}{4}$ hours
5. $\frac{50}{365} = \frac{10}{73}$
Challenge: 586,400 square miles

NUMBER	DIVISIBLE BY ?			
	2	5	9	10
20	yes	yes	no	yes
36	yes	no	yes	no
15	no	yes	no	no
18	yes	no	yes	no
30	yes	yes	no	yes
45	no	yes	yes	no
72	yes	no	yes	no

Worksheet C, page 44
1. $11\frac{3}{5}, 15\frac{7}{9}, 16\frac{7}{10}, 14\frac{5}{12}$
2. $12\frac{1}{3}, 14\frac{7}{15}, 15\frac{7}{12}$
3. $\frac{1}{5}$
4. $3\frac{1}{2}$
5. $\frac{63}{18} = \frac{7}{2} = 3\frac{1}{2}$
Challenge: 1901.0

NUMBER	DIVISIBLE BY ?			
	3	5	9	11
30	yes	yes	no	no
63	yes	no	yes	no
45	yes	yes	yes	no
55	no	yes	no	yes
99	yes	no	yes	yes
144	yes	no	yes	no
33	yes	no	no	yes

Worksheet D, page 45
Answers depend on the numbers placed in left column.

Worksheet E, page 46
1. $\frac{21}{5}, \frac{13}{4}$
2. $\frac{11}{2}, \frac{22}{3}$
3. $\frac{43}{5}, \frac{59}{9}$
4. $\frac{7}{9}, \frac{5}{2}, \frac{2}{3}, \frac{2}{3}$
5. $\frac{1}{4}, \frac{2}{3}, \frac{4}{5}, \frac{1}{2}$
6. 15, 36, 32, 30
7. 40, 35, 20, 70
8. 48, 75, 9, 22

Worksheet F, page 47
1. $10\frac{2}{3}, 5\frac{3}{5}, 16\frac{3}{7}, 16\frac{2}{3}$
2. $9\frac{7}{12}, 7\frac{7}{10}, 11\frac{8}{15}, 17\frac{9}{20}$
3. $4\frac{5}{12}, 9\frac{3}{10}, 10\frac{13}{24}, 16\frac{7}{10}$
4. $18\frac{7}{15}, 22\frac{13}{24}, 22\frac{9}{20}, 20\frac{27}{56}$

Worksheet G, page 48
1. $1\frac{1}{2}, 2\frac{2}{3}, 4\frac{3}{5}, 4\frac{4}{7}, 4\frac{3}{8}$
2. $2\frac{5}{12}, 2\frac{1}{3}, 4\frac{9}{10}, 4\frac{1}{4}, 5\frac{1}{10}$
3. $1\frac{3}{4}, 5\frac{1}{3}, 5\frac{17}{20}, 5\frac{10}{21}, 6\frac{8}{15}$
4. $4\frac{1}{7}, 13\frac{9}{10}, 6\frac{16}{21}, 7\frac{8}{15}, 18\frac{43}{63}$
5. $4\frac{11}{12}, 8\frac{11}{15}, 8\frac{1}{10}, 4\frac{17}{30}, 10\frac{3}{4}$

Worksheet H, page 49
1. $11\frac{3}{5}, 9\frac{2}{3}, 19\frac{5}{7}, 14\frac{7}{9}$
2. $5\frac{7}{12}, 11\frac{7}{10}, 15\frac{8}{15}, 19\frac{9}{20}$
3. $3\frac{2}{5}, 3\frac{3}{7}, 6\frac{4}{9}, 2\frac{1}{3}$
4. $5\frac{3}{4}, 5\frac{1}{3}, 7\frac{1}{3}, 3\frac{3}{10}$
5. $\frac{1}{2}, \frac{3}{4}, \frac{1}{2}, \frac{3}{4}, \frac{2}{3}$
6. $1\frac{1}{2}, 1\frac{3}{4}, 1\frac{1}{5}$
7. $1\frac{1}{5}, 1\frac{5}{7}, 1\frac{1}{3}$

ANSWER KEY

Worksheet I, page 52

1. $\frac{1}{3}, \frac{1}{4}, \frac{2}{5}$
2. $\frac{2}{9}, \frac{3}{5}, \frac{3}{10}$
3. $\frac{1}{3}, \frac{1}{4}, \frac{2}{5}$
4. $\frac{2}{9}, \frac{3}{5}, \frac{3}{10}$
5. $61\frac{7}{10}, 107\frac{5}{12}, 8\frac{1}{5}$
6. $3\frac{7}{12}$ hours
7. $\frac{3}{8}$ of the guests see seals

Challenge: ALYESKA

Worksheet J, page 53

1. $\frac{1}{2}, 2\frac{2}{3}, 13$
2. $1\frac{2}{3}, \frac{1}{2}, 2$
3. $\frac{7}{10}, \frac{1}{4}, \frac{1}{6}$
4. $22\frac{13}{24}, 16\frac{33}{35}, 20\frac{10}{21}$
5. $\frac{4}{5}$ of an hour
6. $2\frac{2}{5}$ hours

Challenge: calving

Worksheet K, page 54

1. $6, 2$
2. $2\frac{3}{4}, 5$
3. $22, 6\frac{4}{7}, 27$
4. $8\frac{5}{12}, 97\frac{7}{16}, 16\frac{5}{6}$
5. $123\frac{7}{24}, 114\frac{7}{20}, 32\frac{1}{6}$
6. $\frac{21}{2}, \frac{57}{8}, \frac{49}{3}$
7. $\frac{49}{9}, \frac{47}{4}, \frac{122}{9}$

Worksheet L, page 55

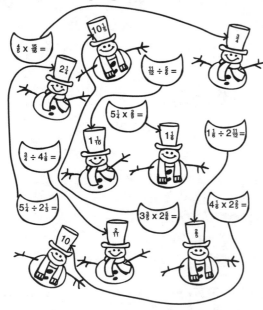

Worksheet M, page 56

1. $16, 7, 10$
2. $3\frac{1}{2}, 13\frac{1}{2}, 12$
3. $\frac{38}{7}, \frac{29}{3}, \frac{49}{8}$
4. $\frac{1}{2}, \frac{3}{4}, \frac{4}{15}$
5. $\frac{1}{2}, \frac{9}{17}, \frac{1}{2}$
6. $1\frac{3}{10}, 2, \frac{9}{10}$
7. $1\frac{37}{75}, \frac{77}{150}, \frac{2}{11}$
8. $\frac{1}{2}, \frac{2}{3}, 1\frac{1}{3}$

Worksheet N, page 57

1. $6\frac{1}{2}, 7$
2. $6, 2$
3. $17, 3$
4. $\frac{3}{4}, 1$
5. $3, 3\frac{1}{2}$
6. $\frac{21}{2}, \frac{57}{8}, \frac{19}{3}$
7. $\frac{49}{9}, \frac{47}{4}, \frac{67}{5}$
8. $\frac{5}{6}, \frac{4}{5}, \frac{4}{5}$
9. $\frac{4}{9}, 3\frac{1}{2}, 3\frac{4}{5}$
10. $\frac{1}{3}, \frac{8}{9}, \frac{1}{15}$
11. $\frac{5}{21}, \frac{3}{13}, \frac{1}{2}$

Worksheet O, page 61

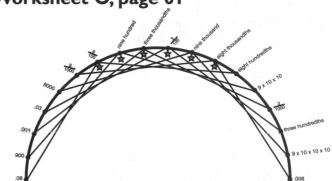

Worksheet P, page 62

1. 325
2. 320.5
3. 300.25
4. .325
5. 3.025
6. 325,000
7. 32.5
8. 32.005
9. 3.25
10. 320.05
11. 1,123.05 + 1,876.95 = 3,000 rivers
12. 1,215,671 + 1,784,329 = 3,000,000 lakes

Challenge: 21,978.6 + 10,689.32 + 332.08 = 33,000 miles in Alaska's coastline

Worksheet Q, page 63

1. $7,200,000
2. 220.009 inches of rain
3. 1397 miles
4. 1.04 persons
5. 80.0008 meters

Challenge: 375,296,000 acres

1	3	9	7			
7	2	0	0	0	0	0
8	0	.	0	0	0	8
2	2	0		0	0	9
			.	1	0	4

Worksheet R, page 64

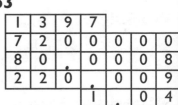

ANSWER KEY

1. 10,250.6
2. 203.24
3. 35,100.08
4. 600,050.009
5. 5,000,020.0004
6. 1 hundred + 2 tens + 3 ones and 4 tenths
7. 5 ten thousands + 4 tens and 3 thousandths
8. 6 millions + 4 thousands + 1 hundred and 2 hundredths
9. 3 ten-thousands + 2 thousands + 6 hundreds and 8 thousandths
10. 2 ten thousands + 3 hundreds + 2 tens
11. 5 hundred thousands + 5 ten thousands + 4 tens + 3 ones

Challenge: 66×10^6 or 6.6×10^7

Decimal Review, page 69

1. 5
2. 4
3. 6
4. 1
5. 23.4
6. .03
7. .50 or .5
8. 123.05
9. 4
10. 20
11. 17.3
12. 16.4
13. 2.74
14. 37.43
15. 1.02
16. 3.88
17. .54
18. 27.28
19. 21.04
20. .9
21. .01
22. 4
23. 2.2
24. $\frac{7}{10}$
25. $\frac{72}{100}$
26. $\frac{75}{100} = 75\%$
27. $\frac{80}{100} = 80\%$
28. .5
29. .2
30. $.87\frac{5}{10}$ or $.87\frac{1}{2}$ or .875

Decimal Pre-Assessment, page 70

1. 3
2. 5
3. 2
4. 7
5. 2.8
6. .04
7. .40 or .4
8. 21.02
9. 10
10. 100
11. 18.1
12. 3.3
13. 11.23
14. 35.83
15. 9.2
16. .94
17. .36
18. 6.75
19. 9.92
20. .5
21. .01
22. 4
23. 2.2
24. $\frac{4}{5}$
25. $\frac{65}{100}$
26. $\frac{60}{100} = 60\%$
27. $\frac{75}{100} = 75\%$
28. .25
29. .7
30. $.62\frac{1}{2}$ or $.62\frac{5}{10}$ or .625

Worksheet S, page 72

1. 12.7, 5.03, 36.0 20.6, 200.9
2. 17.9, 15.8, 32.74, 131.57, 135.04
3. $8\frac{10}{21}$, $67\frac{9}{20}$, $24\frac{23}{30}$, $58\frac{7}{24}$
4. $\frac{3}{5}$, 3, 2
5. 40.83 inches
6. $106.50 for 2 days

Challenge: $1234

Worksheet T, page 73

1. 2.8, 14.9, 87.5 11.29, 5.3, 6.5
2. 5.28, 38.9, 119.73, 133.685
3. $2\frac{1}{2}, \frac{3}{4}, 5\frac{1}{2}$
4. $\frac{1}{3}, 1\frac{3}{10}, 2\frac{1}{8}$
5. 54.88 pounds
6. 368.73 feet

Challenge: $43.21

Worksheet U, page 74

1. $41.16, $28.01, $110.38, $71.40, $395.79
2. 5.6, 16.1, 41.96, 56.13, 55.61
3. 1.75, 14.66, 29.8, 1586.7, 10.942
4. 14.279, 70.33, 45.249
5. 144.861, 48.94, 83.626

Worksheet V, page 75

1. 1.5, 7.5, $1.39, 3.999, 103.9
2. 190.95, $372.91, 10.837, .3588, 11.201
3. 3.078, 216.3, 12.052, 6.085, 212.35
4. 15.888
5. .034
6. 20.583
7. 13.58
8. $84.27
9. 758.738

Worksheet W, page 79

1. 46, 4.6, .46, .046
2. 355, 35.5, 3.55, .355
3. 154, 15.4, .154, 1.54
4. 495, 49.5, .495, .0495
5. 39.6, .396, 29.04, 2.904
6. 959.4, 9.594, 117.64, 1.1764
7. 633.78, 633.78, 6.3378
8. 436.86, 4.3686, .43686
9. 2.4, 3.2, .36
10. 5.0, .016, 7.5

Worksheet X, page 80

1. 70; 700; 80; 8,000
2. 71; 710; 83; 8,300
3. 90; 900; 9,000; 90,000
4. 90; 900; 9,000
5. 100; 100; 100; 100
6. 200; 600; 900
7. 200; 600; 900
8. 700; 800; 500
9. 300; 600; 700
10. 100; 1,000

ANSWER KEY

11. 500; 300; 7,000
12. 4,000; 80,000; 900,000
13. 550; 3,200; 7,200
14. 4,900; 98; 230

Worksheet Y, page 81

1. 5; 50; 5
2. 5.5; 55; 5.50
3. 2; 30; 3
4. .93; .074; .084
5. 800; 3,500; 48,000
6. 7,200; 320,000
7. 21.252; 340.47; 109.668
8. 100,000 glaciers
9. 10^4 volcanoes
Challenge: Arthur Mometer (Our thermometer)

Worksheet Z, page 82

1. 17.5, 8.5
2. 8.4, 41.5, 21.5
3. 12.3, 1.2, 2.1
4. 23, 320, 34

Worksheet AA, page 83

1. $.20 = \frac{20}{100} = \frac{1}{5}$
2. $.5 = \frac{5}{10} = \frac{1}{2}$
3. $.6 = \frac{6}{10} = \frac{3}{5}$
4. $.3, .\overline{16}$
5. $.\overline{1}, .2\overline{7}$
6. 136.8 pounds
7. 527.4 pounds
8. 346.17 miles left

Worksheet BB, page 86

I	P	X	E	D	G	E	A	X	X	
E	G	I	A	N	C	E	T	O	T	
H	E	F	X	A	G	O	F	T	H	
E	U	N	I	T	E	D	S	T	A	
T	E	S	O	F	A	M	E	ⓇR	I	
C	A	A	N	D	T	O	T	H	E	
ⓇR	E	P	U	B	X	I	C	F	O	
ⓇR	W	H	I	C	H	I	T	S	T	
A	N	D	S	O	N	E	N	A	T	
I	O	N	U	N	D	E	ⓇR	G	O	

LETTER	R	S	T	L	N	E
TALLY	IIII	IIII	⊔⊔⊔⊔ I	⊔⊔⊔	⊔⊔⊔ III	⊔⊔⊔ III
RATIO	4/100	4/100	10/100	5/100	8/100	13/100
DECIMAL	.04	.04	.10	.05	.08	.13
PERCENT	4%	4%	10%	5%	8%	13%

Worksheet CC, page 87

1. X = 4; X = 7
2. X = 9; X = 15; X = 24
3. 1,800; 8,000; 2,100
4. 250; 800; 42,000
5. 5.2; 36; 41
6. $\frac{3}{4} = \frac{X}{24}$ X = 18 got frostbite
7. $\frac{60}{100} = \frac{X}{50}$ X = 30 families
Challenge: X = 40 families

Worksheet DD, page 88

NUMBER	10%	1%	1/2%	50%	150%
200	20	2	1	100	300
400	40	4	2	200	600
800	80	8	4	400	1200

1. X = 10, X = 20, X = 30
2. X = 80, X = 70, X = 90
3. $.\overline{6}, .8\overline{3}$
4. 3,000 people
5. 900,000 people
Challenge: 3000 or 3,000 rivers

Fractions Assessment, page 90

1. $1\frac{3}{4}, 3\frac{1}{3}, 22\frac{5}{12}, 15\frac{13}{15}, 15\frac{41}{42}$
2. $\frac{2}{3}, \frac{5}{18}, \frac{1}{12}, 2\frac{7}{8}, 6\frac{9}{20}$
3. $\frac{2}{3}, 1\frac{9}{16}, 1\frac{1}{4}$
4. $\frac{3}{4}, 5\frac{1}{4}, 2\frac{11}{18}$
5. $1\frac{1}{2}, \frac{2}{3}, 30$
6. $\frac{6}{25}, 2\frac{1}{4}, 1\frac{1}{2}$

Decimals Assessment, page 91

1. 44.61, 66.38, 31.41, 131.49
2. 31.78, 234.92, 8.253, 148.03
3. 31.5, 1.16, 20.24, 1.0914, 252.35
4. 9.5, 12.6, 7.3, 20
5. X = 80, X = 10, X = 27
6. 45, 3
7. 1600, 300, 6000
8. 50, .043, $.\overline{3}$
9. $.75, .8, .\overline{83}$

TLC10347 Copyright © Teaching & Learning Company, Carthage, IL 62321-0010